FRUIT
IN THE VINE

Pearl Coleman

New Wine Press

New Wine Press
P.O. Box 17
Chichester
West Sussex PO20 6YB
England

Unless otherwise stated all Bible quotations are from the Authorised Version.

Amplified Bible ©Copyright 1965 Zondervan Publishing House, Grand Rapids, Michigan MI 49506, U.S.A.

ISBN 0 947852 82 4

Typeset by The Ikthos Studios, Chute, Andover, Hampshire, SP11 9DS.

Printed by Richard Clay Ltd. Bungay, Suffolk.

Acknowledgements

This book is dedicated to all those people too numerous to record, who wrote to me concerning my book "Go And Do Likewise" – expressing their thanks and giving me remarkable accounts of how they had been helped by reading it. I have wept over so many of their letters and I am extremely grateful for such encouragement. It has been wonderful to share these numerous incredible testimonies. Thank you in His name from my heart.

Also I wish to thank David and Mary Cleal, who deciphered my awful handwriting and produced the manuscript with a tireless devotion, at the same time as coping with the secretarial work resulting from the deluge of mail from "Go And Do Likewise". Without their labour of love, patience and indeed endurance the presentation of this second book in such a short space of time would not have been possible.

I am so blessed.

Thank you all.

Pearl.

Contents

Foreword

With the flood of Christian books onto the market these days, it is wonderful to read a book which has been clearly written from the heart and based on years of experience.

In writing this book, Pearl Coleman has bared her heart. In so doing she will minister to tens of thousands of people who go through the various trials and tribulations of life. But even more than that, she has exposed in a fresh way the dark and demonic side of evil. Although she is dealing with deep truths, her manner of writing and expression is straightforward and conforms to the simplicity of the Gospel.

Her revelations concerning the manner in which demonic spirits manifest and operate will be a revelation to many.

Her own battles in this realm and the truth the Holy Spirit has taught her as a result of these trials will bless many. I know from my own experience that as we seek to walk with the Lord and proclaim the Gospel of Jesus Christ, we are engaged in a great spiritual warfare. The enemy is ruthless and devious and will use every effort to hinder us from proclaiming the Gospel of the Kingdom of God and Jesus Christ as King.

The encouraging aspect of a book such as this is that, while it deals with these trials and tribulations, nevertheless, it shows that indeed all Christians can triumph in Jesus Christ. He has defeated the enemy at the Cross and has trodden down the prinicipalities and powers. In His name there is victory.

In her humble and self-effacing way, Pearl has again demonstrated this great truth. Her desire to lay down her life completely for Christ comes through with shining clarity.

Once I began reading this book I could not lay it down until I had finished it. I am sure that you too, as you traverse the same paths with Pearl, will see truth demonstrated in a new way and you will be ministered to deeply by the Holy Spirit.

Bill Subritzky
March 1991

Part I

My Healing
And Other Testimonies

Chapter 1

The Accident

To say that I was bubbling over with joy and confidence in the Lord on that beautiful first day of Spring in 1988 is putting it mildly.

Ahead was a busy Clinic day, with patients solidly booked for the next sixteen half hours. I ascended the stairs to my consulting room with the first patient and my Clinical assistant.

We had prayed with the receptionist and secretary before opening the Clinic, giving the day and the work to the Lord as usual, and inviting the Holy Spirit to guide us throughout the patient consultations.

I was hardly upstairs when the telephone rang. I took the call on the consulting room extension, and realized that it was of a personal nature. I called to my secretary that I would take it below stairs.

At that time I was having a sleep problem due, I thought, to my M.E. not then being healed.

I have found that the inability to sleep soundly, although extremely tired, is a common symptom in patients with Myalgia Encephalitis.

My assistant said before the prayers, "When I was praying for you this morning I saw three very clear visions. You, with your head on a brick, unable to sleep, one of those old china jugs and wash basins and a lady in a wheelchair, in black, which could have been you!"

Well, as John Linden-Cook said to me later, "the Word of the Lord to you is WATCH and pray, WATCH and pray, Pearl".

I told the girls that this was most curious because I had one such basin from a jug and basin set purchased from a junk shop when I was formerly married. The jug had cracked some years ago and broken, but the basin was in the shed which backed onto the wall of my bedroom, against which my bedhead rested.

The wisdom of experience has taught me to think twice before purchasing second hand items of dubious antique value and origin. I decided it had to go. As the first patient had arrived we had to move quickly and three of us went out to the shed, smashed it in the name of Jesus and put it in the bin, racing indoors to begin surgery. When in doubt, chuck it out!

Early during the initial consultation I hurried from the consulting room down the stairs to take a telephone call on the office extension. Seconds later I was in a crumpled agonizing heap on my deeply piled Indian carpet in the office below.

I know I let out a wail! My secretary leapt up to assist me, my Clinical assistant rushed downstairs. I was embarrassed because the second patient had arrived early and was sitting in the waiting room!

As one of the girls lifted me up I saw that my hand appeared to be back to front and was very limp. I bravely gave it a quick flick in the ridiculous hope of getting it round the right way and was nearly sick. My secretary gasped in horror as we saw the hand and wrist change before our very eyes.

Of course I was standing on the Word I had called out as I fell.

"He will not suffer my foot to slip, none of my bones shall be broken".

My secretary asked what she could practically do; we were all praying furiously in tongues. I told her to get me to my bathroom where I hosed it with cold water. It just went blue and white becoming even more withered. Well it's no secret that I do not like hospitals, but I was going to have to use one! So bad is my knowledge of

3

such places that first of all I directed my secretary to one which had been closed for two years!

We prayed ceaselessly in the Spirit as we drove. I was coming against the reality of some terrible damage and binding Satan and resisting a spirit of fear. Satan was trying to have a field day and showing me what I thought then was my source of income, the Clinic, cut off and myself – always concerned to be clean – and immaculate, unable to wash! I could not even raise the good arm, such was the nerve-like pain wracking my whole body. What would I do? I lived alone. How could I get my tights on even one-handed? Who would drive me to the shops? The bank? The patients? The car was a lifeline to me. What about the beautiful Clinic garden I was about to plant out? Oh! So many questions all bringing answers which highlighted my helplessness. How indeed could I practice in such pain? I did not think at the time of my assistant being capable of handling everything, which was vanity. She did, bless her heart, although I saw quite a few patients from my bedside as it transpired, even upon my return from hospital that day!

Only when I was in the Outpatients did I look down at my black skirt, shoes and stockings and realise I was in a wheel chair. My blouse was cream with a black pattern on it and my jewellery, jet black beads.

We continued to pray in the Spirit as we waited the hours customary in that particular hospital. Many injured were strewn around the room including a young man who had fallen down an escalator and badly injured his leg. He had two pals with him.

"Are you praying in tongues?" he enquired suddenly.

"Why yes," we responded, "Are you Born Again?" Out came the story. He was a former Satanist saved by the mercies and love of Jesus. I didn't really grasp the story. My hand was hanging down, I was sweating with pain. But I heard God's voice clearly to lay hands on his leg. I was wheeled over and we did this, praying in the Spirit. When it was his turn to go into the doctor

4

before us he got up and walked very easily into the examination room. He was certainly not limping and grimacing as he was when he came in. Praise the Lord!

My anaesthetist was a Moslem. They allowed my secretary to be with me in the theatre following an X-Ray. Nobody was telling me what I had done, only that I would be alright, when the arm was set. Hospitals rarely feel patients want the truth! Especially if it's awful!

"What are you doing?" he queried with regard to our praying in tongues.

"Talking to Jesus," I responded. A Hindu applied a tourniquet and I was given a hideously torturous nerve block injection. A needle was inserted in the back of my other hand which hurt dreadfully. This was apparently the emergency entrance into my veins!

In came a young nurse, looking extremely agitated. He spoke to her. "Never done this before? It's a compound Colles Fracture. Now pull the hand when I say. Turn it round, round. Pull now, pull," and to me, "It will hurt but soon be over and no pain."

We were still praying – myself through clenched teeth. The agony grew worse, it was *not* my imagination. The pain from the blood supply being cut off was a burning undreamed of. I was told that I would feel a burning but not that I should feel I was being roasted alive! I thought of the Christian martyrs at the stake. I did not think I would be as brave as my brothers Ridley and Latimer, who refused to admit the blasphemy of the doctrine of transubstantiation (the bread and the wine being turned into the literal body and blood of Christ) and were murdered by fire at the stake. I still weep for those men, but more so for those who never apologized.

"Please get it straight," I implored as the two of them tugged at it, and finally the plaster was slapped on. It was another three quarters of an hour before they would release the tourniquet. I felt during this ordeal that I would die many times and experienced severe nausea. I was conscious not only of worse pain, but the hideous weight of this very crude plaster of Paris cast.

I asked everyone who checked me over during this time. "What have I done?" But nobody seemed to want to explain. I kept hearing a discussion between staff punctuated by 'very nasty'.

I was alarmed, needless to say, especially when the pain grew worse. I had been promised that I would be pain free by the time I left the hospital, or that it would be nothing a couple of aspirins could not deal with. Nothing could have been further from the truth. I asked to see the casualty consultant.

"Of course it's painful," he barked, "there are a lot of splinters. It's nasty, very nasty."

To his credit he re-x-rayed me and said it was the best they could do and it would settle in a couple of days. It is a good job I believed him at the time.

My secretary drove me back to the Clinic. I was tearful and like a limp rag. In the waiting room was Matthew Larkin, a patient who was healed of terrible psoriatic atrophy and got born again in a powerful way at the Clinic some months earlier. I will never forget how this precious young man took my arm and prayed over it from the Word. He was truly a very anointed young man and I confess to being amazed at his progress in the Spirit. Like myself all those years ago, he had a powerful baptism in the Holy Spirit following giving his life to Jesus and prayed for many hours non-stop in tongues.

He became a very valuable team member and has blessed many in the name of the Lord Jesus. His wife also got born again and they later had a lovely little son. Bless the three of them!

The next chapter tells how he got saved.

Chapter 2

Matthew's Miracle

The Clinic mail always contains a mass of invitations to orthodox and unorthodox medical meetings. We get copious notices of seminars on nutrition taking place country wide, and the inevitable brochures from firms beseeching us to try their latest vitamin or mineral supplements. There is really very little difference between the pressures in the mail here to those I experienced whilst working as Personal Assistant to a General Practitioner when I was also actively pursuing medical journalism. It was common practice to find the surgery door jammed in the morning by mail from drug companies entreating the recommendations of their particular brand of whatever!

One simply has to get a larger waste paper basket for such mail – and so it is at the Clinic nowadays. The ministry does not allow time wasting on such matters. I do always glance at most things and one becomes an expert at recognizing envelopes which have to go into the bin unopened.

So it was at the particular time that I found myself unable to throw away the details of a seminar on nutrition at Gatwick. The fees for the two days attendance were quite exorbitant. That in itself should have constituted a reason for the disposal of their papers. However, the Holy Spirit had other plans and the papers for this meeting constantly surfaced at the top of the pile on my desk.

Finally I gave them to two of my staff.

"I cannot seem to throw these away and it's ridiculously expensive. Pray about it please".

When I came downstairs from my consulting room

they both called out with one voice of conviction that I should definitely book in. So I did.

As I have written often, there is no such thing as a coincidence. All is God-incidence in my life. Thus it was that I found myself at the conference sitting next to a dentist puffing away with his Ventolin inhaler. I challenged him.

"What are you doing with that thing?"

"Well I have asthma, I've used it for twenty years".

"That's twenty years too long," I replied, "Anyway asthma is quite curable. I expect you've got Candidosis?"

"What's that?"

"It's a yeast mould problem. Write to me and I'll send you information on it. It causes a wide range of symptoms and disease states from warts and athletes foot, to rheumatoid and osteoarthritic disease, Crohn's and ulcerative colitis, psoriasis, eczema, acne, etc."

I tossed him my card. We had a couple of chats at meal breaks, when I was able to advise him that he was eating all the wrong things, and he came to see me at the Clinic a couple of weeks later.

The root of his asthma proved to be fear and guilt, but he had an established respiratory disease. Again we used the diet, also deliverance. He learned the discipline of not eating junk food (as I described in my book "Go And Do Likewise"), and gave his life to Jesus, coming off his medication after all those years. He found a good fellowship, received the gift of tongues, got baptized by immersion, and is now studying the scriptures and telling others about Jesus. He also proved a great help in our team.

Shortly after his treatment and before he found Jesus, one of his own dental patients became severely ill with psoriatic atrophy. This gentleman was Matthew. His blood pathology gave an E.S.R. (erythrocyte sedimentation rate) of 114 and many joints especially one knee were swollen and painful.

His back and more especially his scalp, forehead and

ears were erupting with hideous crusts. The skin was scarlet and the lesions moist and scaly. He was to be admitted to hospital and I believe rang to cancel his dental appointment due to this fact.

However his dentist, newly impressed by his deliverance from Ventolin, recommended that he visited the Clinic at Woking.

I saw him on 11.5.87. He returned on 28.5.87 with his doctor's notes. He had told me his E.S.R. was now 15, the hospital admission was cancelled. His G.P. was amazed and said something like.

"I don't know what you've done but clearly it works!"

Again, we had tested Matthew, found he suffered from Candidosis, so he went onto the correct diet and recovered. Matthew told me that he did meditate 'to help reduce stress,' and I told him that I hoped that he didn't mean Transcendental Meditation.

Before he left the Clinic he challenged me.

"What's wrong with T.M.? Isn't it for stress? I have practised it for stress. I thought it was a good thing".

"No wonder you get sick", I told him, "The practice is occult, you need to confess and repent it without delay. Then the spirit of T.M. needs to be called out in the name of Jesus." Matthew looked afraid.

"How can I do that?"

I told him that we could do it there and then. He only vaguely knew Jesus, but was very eager to get free. To my astonishment he was slain in the Spirit. As he lay there I called out the spirit of fear in the name of Jesus and was led by the Holy Spirit to break the curse of poverty over his life. Before I did so I enquired if he had money problems and he stated emphatically that he did.

His deliverance was followed up listening to Christian cassettes by Derek Prince on demons and deliverance. He asked me to get him the Bible I thought most suitable and he began to study the Word of God, always going home with a pile of books from our library and going through our teaching cassettes like a dose of salts.

At the first Clinic teach-in he attended, (his dentist also came), John Linden-Cook was the guest speaker. They both gave their lives to Jesus and have never looked back. We have witnessed a heartening spiritual growth in them both and the team has received much support from them. Matthew is studying the Foundation Series of Bible Teaching by Derek Prince Ministries.

Praise the Lord! That's why He sent me to that conference on nutrition at Gatwick! As a result two men tasted their first spiritual food!

Chapter 3

Black Despair

My arm had to be strapped above my head and I was warned not to let it hang down. Living on my own, this was impossible to do. The pain under the weighty plaster was like being in an iron maiden. It felt as though iron spikes were being crushed into my flesh. I was chalk white and weak. A kind neighbour started to come over at night and prop it up high wedged in many pillows. The nights of pain were hell!

Reading my Bible and playing cassettes to encourage myself was not easy because the slightest movement sent the pain all over my body. I lay there thinking what manner of injury this could be. Brother Ernest from my team ferried me on alternate days to the fracture Clinic where I begged them to ease the pain. I was told to take pain killers, but since they afforded no relief and I was aware of their side effects I saw no point in drugging myself. My fingers projecting through the end of the cast began to tingle and get numb. I constantly pointed this out at the hospital and at one point the plaster was loosened. Pain under my armpit was intense.

My secretary and clinical assistant slept on the floor beside my bed for the first few nights following my injury, but both having small children and living miles away, this could not go on. But Cheril, bless her, came in to dress me on Clinic days, and somehow trying to cover up the pain and not confess it, I managed with the help of my assistant to see patients. I had to because at that time I could not see my security of income other than in my work. The Lord was to change all that!

11

In common with many stories related to me by my patients, I started to row with the consultants at the hospital, who clearly thought me a cissy, making a fuss about nothing. All the time I was getting so exhausted that I was actually struggling for survival and constantly wondering how I could meet the mortgage and overheads if I succumbed. The peak of my despair came in a terrible blackness one night. My neighbour had propped me up. I knew that there were many who had prayed and were praying for me. Intercession was intense for my healing. But the heavens were as brass. I had finally succumbed to morphine but I just got nauseous and retched. This jolted my whole body and exacerbated the agony. I called out to God with a loud voice. No answer! I called out again. No answer! I had been speaking the Word out "*by His stripes I am healed,* not to be healed, *am healed,*" until it seemed just a mockery. I felt my faith ebbing away.

I had laid aside so much to follow Jesus. How could God do this to me? I constantly reminded Him of the Covenant. All to no avail. I got in agreement with His Word, all to no avail! I realize that many Christians reading this will identify in their various dilemmas! A blackness descended over me and as it swamped me, unseen hands rolled my duvet around me and over my head. In spite of the terrible pain in my arm I struggled in a life and death struggle. I was suffocating. Who was this? How did they get into the Clinic? I had to leave the back door unbolted in the day so someone could get to me in an emergency, but it was locked at night.

Had a stranger got in and hidden themself on a non Clinic day and was now attacking me? The duvet was wrapped tighter and tighter around me, I was sweating with fear. Suddenly I realized it was a spiritual warfare. With all the strength I could muster I gasped JESUS! JESUS! JESUS!

I continued to repeat his name, gaining strength with each utterance, until finally the tightness of the duvet coiled around me like a fat serpent loosened. I kicked my leg out of it and disentangled myself. I sat up in bed and wept with relief. I felt very confused. Was this the effect of various strong pain killers. Did I imagine it all? Was it a nightmare?

Chapter 4

Revelation

I did not return to sleep that night but sat up reading the Psalms of Praise. I still felt very ill and wracked with pain but I knew Satan that Prince of Darkness had been overcome. I felt I had been wrestling against some principality or power.

Ernest rang me in the morning as he did every day. Ernest is seventy seven. His wife Renie was one of our precious counsellors. After she died the Lord told Ernest to stand with me, pray for me and support me. He has done just that.

Of course in about five minutes flat many Christians wanted to marry us off! One really despairs at the matchmaking, sometimes. It's not helped by the fact that Ernest has been a patient of mine, done the diet and in common with many veteran patients shed about twenty years. So he's often taken for my husband although I have no wedding ring to encourage people to believe this. Looking about the same age causes many to put two and two together and make ten! I never had unconditional Christian love from a man until I met Ernest. There's been plenty since from the husbands of my sisters in Christ and other single Christian men, but Ernest was the first to show me this kind of support. He has blessed me.

So when he called me that morning saying he had to come and see me, it was not easy for me to say that he could not do so. Strangely for Ernest he pressed his request home. "I must speak to you Pearl, I cannot do it over the telephone. I must talk to you face to face."

"I'm sorry Ernest. I cannot see anyone. I feel ill, the pain is worse and I've had such a bad night I cannot cope. I cannot wash, I'm sweaty and smelly and I cannot move".

Fully expecting him to say 'alright dear!' I confess I was astonished when he seemed to weep at the other end of the telephone. So I found myself saying it was alright, but that he couldn't stay long and that I was a disgusting sight.

As a woman who has always taken a pride in her appearance, this experience of disability was very humbling and humiliating.

I crawled out of bed, cleaned my teeth and tried to wash under my arms with the plaster cast above my head. You try as you read this. Put your left arm up. Imagine a sack of cement on it. Take a flannel with your right hand rub it on the soap and wash under your right armpit with it. Even while you are not in agony it's not easy.

My disability heightened my awareness of the misery and the overcoming that handicapped people are involved in. How I have marvelled at some of the ingenious ways they manage to overcome appalling difficulties. What a trifle my injury was in comparison. How grateful I should be to have one good arm.

We all know, of course, that somebody else's worse suffering is of no comfort in our own personal agony! However I gained a deeper and more real compassion for the disabled in my wretchedness. That is certain.

The moment Ernest entered the bedroom I could detect that he was different. His face was as red and glowing as a sunset. He was clutching his Bible and a piece of paper.

"What is it Ernest?" I enquired.

"Last night I went to bed as usual at about ten o'clock. I said my prayers and fell asleep. As you know I usually sleep like a top, but at about one o'clock in the morning I was awakened by myself praying in a very loud and strange tongue. It was so fast and strong, it was not my

15

usual tongue. The Lord told me to get up and pray. I slid out of bed, my mouth was so dry my tongue ached, it was moving so fast. I made sure to look at the clock.

I prayed for about an hour when suddenly I was transported in the Spirit to the Clinic. I found myself with my back against the consulting room window looking out at the garden. I could clearly see the bird bath, the bird table and the boundary hedge. My feet were astride the whole grounds. I felt as if each one was placed on a spiritual wall".

By this time tears were streaming down Ernest's face, and he took the piece of paper he had placed on his Bible. He had to calm himself.

"A voice, I know it was the Lord, spoke to me so clearly. It was not faint and it was a command. I wrote it down as soon as I could, I felt it was so important." He read out from the piece of paper.

"STAND ASTRIDE THE CITY OF GOD WHICH IS MY DAUGHTER'S HOUSE AND WARD OFF THE POWERS OF DARKNESS."

He continued, "I found myself with my legs astride this spiritual wall, pushing out against a mighty force. During the second hour of praying in the Spirit I thought I should telephone someone. I considered this several times but was commanded to pray on.

The danger seemed to subside and I was kept praying at intervals until 4am, then at lesser intervals until about 6am when I was exhausted.

Later in the morning when I read what I had written there was a space and I had written two words, 'The devil.' I believe that was after I had such a desire to ring someone, and stop praying in the Spirit. My tongue was dry."

I was able to check out the times with my own dreadful experience that night and clearly it was a battle against the powers of darkness.

Chapter 5

Rescue

I owe the fact that I have an arm at all to Jenny Maylem who called to see me on Good Friday. She found me in a desperate state and I demonstrated that I could not feel my fingers. She rang my G.P. He was out, but a locum came. I was immediately admitted to hospital.

At casualty outpatients I saw the Indian doctor who set my arm. He looked flustered. A young English doctor was called in and he quickly cut the plaster away. Even then I had no idea how serious the injury was. All I know is that since the arm could not be set by this time, I was told not to move it as it rested in the slit open plaster cast.

I screamed. It was withered. The doctor reluctantly admitted that the plaster was too tight and said he would operate and cut the nerve to see if the circulation would return.

"No!" I exclaimed, "I do not want surgery. Please, please let me see if I can wiggle it and get the circulation back without an operation."

"Alright, since we are short-staffed as it is Easter we'll leave you overnight and if you do not succeed we'll operate tomorrow."

I took only three things into hospital, my dressing gown (I was wearing my nightie), my toilet bag and my Bible. I did not even take my journalist's note book which would normally accompany me everywhere. I own four Bibles. This was my small original now tatty King James. I made certain that the nurse put it on the bed where I could reach it.

I lay there entreating the Lord to make my circulation return. I prayed without ceasing in tongues for hours as I awaited my fate. I entreated the Lord for a scripture and was given Jeremiah 1:18-19:

'FOR, BEHOLD, I HAVE MADE THEE THIS DAY A DEFENCED CITY, AND AN IRON PILLAR, AND BRASEN WALLS AGAINST THE WHOLE LAND, AGAINST THE KINGS OF JUDAH, AGAINST THE PRINCES THEREOF, AGAINST THE PRIESTS THEREOF, AND AGAINST THE PEOPLE OF THE LAND. AND THEY SHALL FIGHT AGAINST THEE; BUT THEY SHALL NOT PREVAIL AGAINST THEE; FOR I AM WITH THEE, SAITH THE LORD, TO DELIVER THEE.'

I was so encouraged I fell asleep. When I awoke I thought to read that scripture again to comfort myself. My head felt as if it was on a brick. I could not get the feeling of my pillow soft. As I complained to a nurse she said "Oh yes, I know we are so short of linen and pillows, I expect it's stuffed with horse hair!"

She inspected it and confirmed that this was so.

"It's so hard," I moaned, "It feels as if my head is on a brick."

As I said those words I recalled my receptionist's vision. The three signs. The woman in black in a wheelchair, one with my head on a brick and the old fashioned china washing bowel and jug. I gasped. I wanted to read Jeremiah again for comfort. The nurse was attempting to soften my pillow, "My Bible, where is my Bible?" I exclaimed. My arm was slung up high in a special chair sling on a pulley in the open cast, so my movement was extremely limited. I fumbled in the bed clothes, looked on the bedside locker, all to no avail. The nurse was searching too and questioning me whether I was certain I had it nor not. I was very upset.

"Of course I had it. I had been reading it before I fell asleep. I said it was not to be removed, where is it? Find it please!"

Now we were joined by another nurse. We all searched in vain. I felt an evil presence and started to pray quietly in the Spirit.

My bed was situated outside the glass panelled office which is usually central to most N.H.S. wards, and houses the ward sister's desk and file and place for the Staff nurse. I became aware of the Staff nurse rising to her feet behind the glass partition and heading for my bed. She approached haughtily to discover what the fuss was about. Our eyes met.

I was coming face to face with a spiritualist. It was warfare!

"My Bible has gone," I spoke boldly. "I want it found." She tried to make out that I must have imagined having it as she pretended to search the covers and under the bed. Now four nurses were looking. My spiritual antennae were up. All the time I was praying in tongues. This clearly made her uncomfortable. She opened the locker drawer stating that it was not there. I was still in terrible pain but with as much strength as I could muster I called out: "In the name of Jesus Christ, find my Bible! I will not be quiet until it is found."

Everyone looked shocked. Other patients were beginning to stir. Suddenly this staff nurse bent down, opened the back bottom entrance to the locker and retrieved my Bible. Remember, I had no luggage, no possessions with me. Why was it not popped in the empty locker drawer? Or even placed on the top? She handed it to me with an evil grin. I knew what she was, and she knew that I knew.

I had to submit to emergency surgery on Easter Saturday. In spite of drugs being put under my tongue and injections for pain I knew no physical peace.

When I came to after the anaesthetic I could not believe the pain and I was back in a sealed, hideously heavy plaster. I entreated them to change it for a honeycomb plaster but was told that there was no substitute for plaster of Paris.

"But this plaster is so tight also," I told the house surgeon. "Look at my fingers, they are numb and going blue again."

I was terrified. Already I had a dead arm. I kept protesting. Finally the surgeon produced a Swiss Scout Knife and hacked away at the end where my blue fingers protruded, so I could try to wriggle my thumb.

I could fill pages with the horror of my time there. The two night nurses were spiritualist mediums. As I was alert in warfare throughout the night, not daring to sleep although I often pretended to, I could hear their occult utterances. They treated me with cold disdain, especially when I wanted the bed pan. I was still restricted by the high chair sling. During this time some sort of raffle was being organized by the sister. The prizes were placed on a table quite near my bed. This first prize was a china wash bowl and jug!! A very pretty modern replica of the antique type!

On Easter Sunday a nurse announced, "Who wants Holy Communion?"

"I do," I said, sitting bolt upright. She sailed down the ward, continuing her announcement.

"All those who want Communion will have to go into the next room."

This I gathered was a lounge attached to the ward and contained armchairs, a table with magazines on and a colour T.V. Sundays is always a bleak day with a scarcity of nursing staff in any hospital. Easter Sunday or any Bank Holiday was even worse. I sought help to be unstrapped from the hoist but none came. The ward was as silent as the grave.

Praying in the Spirit I made a superhuman effort to unstrap my arm. I finally succeeded. I grabbed my Bible, and binding the fear of falling I slowly tottered into the side room. What confronted me was horrific. Remember, I was in an orthopaedic ward. The seats had been pushed into a row facing a large colour T.V. on a centre table. They were, in the main, a row of elderly badly injured or crippled old ladies. One slightly younger lady had horrific stitching to her shaven head. It transpired that she had been thrown from a pony and trap when her horse bolted. Her brain was affected.

Hardly having taken in this picture of infirmity, (and trying to hold my plaster cast up and hold my Bible and not trip over my dressing gown put on badly because I could only get one arm in a sleeve, so it hung on me very low down and I could not tie it up), I became aware that those gathered were glued to the television, which I disconnected in favour of reading Isaiah 61 to the amazed row of ladies. Then I went along the line, my damaged arm now had to hang down, laying hands on each person and praying in the Holy Spirit. I did not reach the end of the line before a large lady, gowned in cream brocade entered like a prize battleship.

"Ah! I see you are deputizing for me," she said as she took over.

I stepped back to my end of the line to receive Communion from this very strange lady, who sailed past with the cup and wafers. I took Communion and prayed quietly. When I opened my eyes, I was in time to see that the evil looking staff nurse had slipped in and joined the line. She put the cup to her lips and as she returned it to the robed personage she spoke in a loud voice.

"Of course, I'm from the Spiritualist Church."

I cursed the Spiritualist Church in Jesus' name and went back to bed. Two days later I was discharged.

Chapter 6

Dismissed

After five days of severe pain and more rows at the fracture Clinic I told a consultant that I wanted another opinion. He told me that he would be glad to see the back of me because I'd been nothing but trouble since I arrived.

I rang the clinic medical adviser and he was very concerned. He got me an appointment at a Private Hospital. Out of courtesy I informed the consultant at the fracture Clinic at my last visit and asked if he had any objections.

"Certainly not," he replied, "I'm glad to get rid of you."

I gritted my teeth. "Then I'll take my X-Rays", I said, "I've already had too much radiation."

To my astonishment he replied, "Fine, that's if we can find them, it's chaotic around here."

That was the only thing we could agree on. Each time I attended the fracture Clinic my X-Rays were missing. Ernest and I prayed each time we waited for me to be seen but they were lost temporarily. One began to feel nervous! Clutching my X-Rays Ernest drove me home. I could not wait to scan the X-Rays. I was so shocked. It was a very unusual Colles fracture with the break in the radius much higher than usual. The styloid was severed from the ulna which was very severely splintered. The radius was also badly splintered with one very large splinter indeed. The many little bones in the bracelet area where the wrist joins the hand were very indistinct. I was told later that they were pulled and fused together. My hand looked clubbed for many months.

I had a horrible feeling as I gazed at the X-Ray that I must have a bone disease.

My treatment at this Private Hospital was a dream compared with the nightmare of my treatment at the N.H.S. hospital. There is not a shadow of doubt in my mind that the wonderful and compassionate consultant I saw was absolutely horrified, both at the state of the plaster of Paris, the weight of it and the cobbling of the surgical incision. The medical profession are known to stick together, but this man was definitely on my side.

I soon learned the horrific cost of X-Rays and dressings, but was prepared to spend my last penny for correct treatment. We shall see later what God did about this.

At every turn however, I found the mercy of God in peculiar provision. I owe a great debt to John Matthews, the born-again physio from Guildford. Again here was a man of God who gave me Jesus' love and compassion and a Godly encouragement that I could use the hand again. I kept asking him what the prognosis was. Would I ever drive again? He said he hoped that I would, but in all his experience, (and believe me it was vast) he had not seen a similar injury. When he was on holiday he left his colleague to treat me in his absence. I was very perturbed to find that when he saw my X-Rays, he was unwilling to manipulate my arm at all!

By the time I got my appointment to see the No. 1 in Britain hand fracture man, the movement of the limb had so improved that surgery was postponed, but I was still paralysed to the degree that I could barely grip.

Chapter 7

The Snare Of The Fowler

On one of his teaching tapes Derek Prince describes how Satan knows our every activity and follows us throughout each day. I write too in the introduction to this book of the plots and plans of the wicked.

When one suffers such a complicated and hideous injury from a simple fall, one is met by the incredulity of the inquisitive that one did not fall from a great height. It was frequently assumed that I fell down the stairs – which I did not. It is also important to report that one of my staff also almost slipped on the identical spot that same morning.

I was aware before the accident of John Linden-Cook's advice to watch and to pray – and I have nobody except myself to blame that I chose to be deaf and dismissive of a warning which may have saved me so much pain.

The Clinic floors are all pine which have been sealed with a preparation used on yachts. No polishes, sprays or chemicals of any kind are used in the cleaning of the Clinic for obvious reasons.

If the seal gets damaged or scratched around the carpets, which are all white deeply piled Indian carpets, the damaged area would be treated with a preparation which fills in scratch marks on wooden surfaces. There would be no point in applying the liquid except to a damaged surface area because it would simply sit on the pine sealer, not be absorbed and therefore be very slippery and dangerous.

There would therefore be no occasion to put any such treatment on areas under rugs or carpets because those places being protected by carpeting would never get damaged.

On the Friday prior to the Monday Clinic, when the Clinic was being clinically ecologically cleaned, I had removed two white Indian rugs exactly below the stairs. After twenty years hard wear they needed replacing. They were not easy to replace but I finally located a pair in a large chain store I had done business with over some thirty years.

I explained carefully that they must arrive immediately the cleaning was carried out and delivery was agreed for that Friday morning.

I disposed of the worn rugs and instructed the cleaner, a new and very fearful lady, to watch out for the van, to clean the floor and treat the scratched area around the edge of where the rugs would be put down.

I should say that when this lady joined us she was very interested in the Holy Spirit and subsequent to joining us got baptized in the Holy Spirit and was delighted to receive the gift of tongues. She also got busy with her Bible for the first time in her life. However, this created the most appalling difficulties with her atheist spouse at home, and he began to put pressure on her to leave. I saw him a couple of times briefly and he clearly had very severe demonic problems and felt very threatened by the very existence of myself and the Clinic. It was a classic example of a spirit recognizing what is in a believer and wanting to move away fast! I sensed an incredible hatred and resentment of me from this man, although I was naturally always greeting him with the love of Jesus shed abroad in my heart.

I gathered that my cleaner did actually drag him along to her church sometimes, a church where the Holy Spirit was clearly moving.

Well, we kept listening for the car that morning and she was concerned that the driver may not find the Clinic. I assured her that he would as they had called often over the years. I was working at the opposite end of the building and I kept thinking, "Whatever is she doing down there, taking all that time on the pine floor?" Doing the scratches once the area had been cleaned with vinegar and water should have been a five minute job.

Suddenly she leapt to her feet crying out, "I saw the van. Shall I go down the lane and direct them? They've gone past."

"Good gracious, Susan," I insisted, "for heaven's sake don't panic, the driver knows exactly where we are, I expect he's turning the van around at the end of the lane." Well, they did not arrive, and two hours later I rang the store to find that they had searched and could not find us. It was a different driver! I felt very stupid and apologized to Susan (not her real name). She was still fiddling below the stairs. I wondered what on earth she was up to but one never inspects good cleaning ladies, because they leave and are difficult to replace!

So Susan went home and I gazed at the awful blank floor. Fortunately I was out most of the weekend and did not have to look at it. The store promised to come early the next week. I would only have to manage without cover for a day. I knew what I would do. We had some strips of ridged heavy duty plastic carpet protection. The side which should grip a fitted carpet had little teeth in it to press into the pile.

I would simply lay it so the teeth would not scratch the boards. I dumped a couple of strips over the area and forgot about it.

I want you to note the sequence of these events, which illustrates my error in not watching in every respect, and taking too many things for granted due to habit.

I did not have to tread that way until Sunday night when I sat down at the long table in the dining room, below the stairs which was converted on Mondays into the office, to do some writing.

At weekends I always went barefoot. My first book "Go and Do Likewise", was at that time being compiled and spread all over the end of the table.

I sat down at about 8.30pm to write a couple of chapters. At nine o'clock the telephone rang, I was aggravated, but got up to reply. It was Susan.

"I saw you slip," she said, "be careful, you ought to check the foot of the stairs."

"Nonsense, Susan," I replied. "Last week you were afraid that the curtain rail was going to fall down. The week before you thought that a picture hanger was loose. We really must pray about that spirit of fear! When are you going to let us do that?"

"Not yet. But I actually saw you fall, please be careful."

"I will, darling," I replied cheerfully, eager to get back to my writing. "Just you stop worrying and pop off to bed."

I put the telephone down, thinking what a silly old fearful sweetie she was and without a second thought got my head down over my manuscript. The telephone rang a second time. Susan repeated her fears, which I again dismissed and returned to my writing.

As it transpired the whole area below the plastic had been treated with the scratch remover and it sat on the sealant like ice. To make matters worse I chose that dreadful Monday to wear a brand new pair of black leather sandals which had shiny new leather soles, a rare occurrence these days for uppers and soles both to be real leather.

Satan observed me all the way. I am certain of that.

I awoke from my pain early in the days of disaster to find Susan sobbing as she knelt at my bedside, her head on the counterpane.

"What have I done? The devil told me to kill you. I tried to warn you – but you would not listen. You must believe what I say."

"Nonsense, Susan," I replied, "you are always worrying and –." But I stopped in my tracks. I looked at her ashen, wretched, pleading face.

"Oh God! Oh God!" I cried out, "Oh God!"

Years later I have learned that Susan was finally edged out of the Clinic by her husband whom she feared, and she no longer uses the gift of tongues or reads her Bible. She has also left her fellowship for an "old fashioned type of Church" – in which it appears there is no moving of the Holy Spirit. And she feels more comfortable.

Chapter 8

More Plots And Plans Of The Wicked

I had been pretty frantic turning over in my mind and praying with desperation to know what I could do to speed up the process of healing, and to piece together the pieces in the jigsaw of my injury, as I lay night after night with the feeling that iron splinters were tearing into my arm, wrist and hand.

On one Clinic day during this period a new patient, a professional polo player, had booked in for treatment. By this time I was not so embarrassed about making a bad first-time impression being in plaster.

As I studied this young man's notes – I read 'Broken hip, broken legs, repeated broken arms, hands, collar bones, etc, etc.' I was quite aghast at the catalogue of injuries.

"Why, you must have broken nearly every bone in your body, more than once!" I exclaimed. "How is it that you walk so well? Why do you continue to play?"

"It's in my blood I suppose," he responded. "My horses also get injured, but I go to see Sadie (not her real name) and she puts me right with her machine which unites bad fractures painlessly and in double-quick time. She treats my horses also."

My heart leapt! I enquired as to her whereabouts.

"You look as if you could do with her yourself," the young man went on.

He gave me an address in the salubrious area of medical residences in London. I could not think why as a medical journalist I did not know about her or the machine. I was told that she had treated the Royal family, (Princess Margaret was mentioned) and a very famous jockey who broke his back racing, but that they did not want publicity as she was not accepted by the profession. She also claimed to heal burns with this device. Well, of course, I did not pooh pooh it, having an open but very cautious investigative mind on such matters.

I came down stairs and gave my receptionist her London telephone number to ring urgently to speak with her. I said to my astute secretary.

"Oh! Isn't it hopeful? Could be a miracle?"

She replied "Either it's a miracle, or it is Satan."

That remark sobered me up a little and I returned to see the next patient awaiting me upstairs. Meanwhile Helen tried many times unsuccessfully to contact the number. That coming weekend was yet another Bank Holiday and I wanted desperately to try and locate this machine before then. Anything to speed up my mobility.

I found myself at about 8pm on the telephone, my head was almost on the telephone table with pain and exhaustion, when I got through.

The voice was pleasant. I imagined a lady in her late forties or fifties, not very professional. I explained who I was, that I was a committed Christian and the nature of my injury. These electrical machines I was told cost £5,000 each but one could hire them. None was available at that particular time, and she was off with her son for the Bank Holiday and could not therefore deliver one even if she had one to hand. They were all out on loan and in short supply.

To my remarks of not knowing about her she gave logical and plausible replies. There had been quite a lot of prestigious name-dropping of the famous whom she had treated with her machine, up to that point in our conversation.

As she was speaking I felt that I recognised this homely sort of voice. It had a ring of familiarity – and of course by this time in my horrific experience my guard was up and I *was* watching!

The moment I explained to her that I was a medical journalist and had had my own columns in three magazines in the past as well as being a house journalist, she got very interested. I realized immediately that she had twigged that she could use me to get publicity.

"Leave it with me, dear, I'll ring my son and call you back."

"I thought you were off for the Bank Holiday?" I queried suspiciously.

"Yes dear, but you are obviously in severe pain. I'll call you back as soon as I get hold of him."

By this time I was extremely exhausted by pain. Normally I would go straight to bed after a Clinic day. I sat very tired at the telephone desk in the hall with my head down and my plastered arm uncomfortably on the desk. I almost fell asleep. Every part of my body ached with tension, especially my neck and shoulders. I had learned to tuck the receiver uncomfortably under my chin so I could write with my right arm. The telephone rang about forty minutes later. I put the receiver to my ear without raising my head off the table. As I heard her voice I sat bolt upright. Large and evil in front of my bleary tired eyes I saw in the Spirit a two headed cobra. I blinked. Yes, it was still there.

She was chatting on about how she and her son would drop a machine in to me at the weekend. I need not pay, but she would like publicity.

"Wait," I said. "Are you a medium?"

She replied that she was, and it only remained for me to tell her that I was not interested in her wonder machine, and to cut myself off from her in the name of Jesus and phone a couple of the saints to pray likewise over me! I gave her Deuteronomy 18:10-13.

Wait until I saw that polo player! He was in real trouble!

He did not come again, and neither did the lady patient

31

who recommended him as a patient. What is more, out of sheer curiosity I tried to locate him, but both he and she simply melted away. Try as I might, I could not trace either of them at either of the addresses given.

What a spiritual warfare!

Chapter 9

Ministry At The Old Mill

Try as I might, the frustration of waiting for the bones in my arm to set and the pain was tormenting me. My whole body knew no peace because of the internal splinters not yet dissolved by macrophages. The tightness and weight of the plaster in what was incredible spring weather added to my discomfort. As a person who had daily completed a workout for many years and been fit and tuned, I soon became flabby and unfit, disliking myself more by the minute! I found it difficult to fix my hair with one hand. Normally I washed my hair daily, I showered daily – and all this was a nightmare because I was forbidden to wet the plaster.

My wardrobe was confined to clothes I could step into, and most miserable of all for me was not being able to wear a bra, because it could not be fastened. I went through model school in my twenties and certainly retained the discipline of grooming and matching!

I had a very beautiful bedroom which was my prayer sanctuary – even this looked as if it had been sandbagged to keep the arm suspended above my head.

Losing the independence of driving was another blow, and when I left the hospital that Easter, Ernest insisted he take me out to tea. I protested that I wanted to crawl away and hide, but he persisted.

The only place where I felt I could tuck myself away as the waitresses had known me for two decades, was The Old Mill at Gomshall.

So I allowed Ernest to drive me there. I did not want to eat but I knew a salad would do me good. I had eaten little decent food since the injury.

I was horrified when we entered, to find the place swarming with mothers and children. Of course it was the Easter Holiday. I made to rush out. I was expecting the calm peace and tranquility usually found there.

Ernest restrained me. The waitress exclaimed, "Oh, dear Pearl, what have you done?" I was guided to a seat I did not wish to sit at, but honestly there was no choice. Very disgruntled I sat down, giving apologetic explanations to the inquisitive and horrified staff who knew me extremely well, and also gave me excellent service. Actually I did not want sympathy, but just to hide and leave as quickly as possible. Everyone gets dressed up for Easter. I felt I would have looked better in a sack!

We ordered our snack and in spite of my misery my eyes were drawn to a boy of about six who sat at a table opposite us and to the right. I could never have had this vantaged viewpoint had I not been seated in this particular corner.

The mother's back was towards us. Her stature was that of a Chinese and her small boy was obviously a mixture. He had dark skin and outstanding were his coal black eyes. His thumb was permanently in his mouth and he was sucking frantically and looking at me. I waved and smiled. With his free hand he waved back. I nudged Ernest.

"Look at the spirit of fear in that child, Ernest," I implored. "He has a thumb sucking spirit, which is a fear spirit."

Ernest agreed. The child kept on looking over at our table as though fascinated. I leaned across and waved at him.

"Agree with me and bind it Ernest." We agreed, prayed and the child's hand fell out of his mouth. I beckoned him over to sit next to me. But he leaned over, his coal black eyes staring and said fearfully, "I cannot speak to strangers."

I leaned over towards where he was sitting, speaking so that his mother could hear. She turned around quickly.

"I'm not really a stranger and it is quite safe to speak to me when mummy is with you."

I saw him obtain permission from his mother to join us and he slid out of his seat and came and perched next to me like a little bird. His eyes were so dark. There were no shades in the iris. They shone like black coal. We struck up such an interesting conversation. He questioned me about how many times I had visited the Old Mill as he had not seen me before – and did I like cakes because he did? And where was I going after my tea?

I explained carefully about the rule of not talking to strangers, that if he was with mummy in a crowded place like this tea room it was perfectly safe, but if alone in the street or a shop it may not be.

The spirit of fear in him was so strong and evident I was longing to get at it. When he returned to his seat, his shirt came away from his pants. Either he had a nappy on or a plaster. I pointed this out to Ernest.

"That child has something peculiar about his back, Ernest". Ernest had not noticed.

I was very attracted to this bright little conversationalist.

I could not let him get out of the tea room without telling his mother the good news concerning spirits of fear. I wanted also to give her some gentle advice on not making this dear child fearful.

They had to pass us to get out and in spite of my arm I reached out and restrained her. She turned round. I loved Gail on sight. She was a beautiful lady. I handed her my card, talked about her son Peter's fear and she glanced at the card noting the cross and dove motif.

"Oh! You are a born-again Christian, so am I."

"My, we're in business," I thought, and soon Peter was sitting opposite me next to Ernest and Gail was by my side. Born-again Christians always meet like old friends. I could feel the presence of the Holy Spirit in Gail as she told us about Peter. She was a single parent and Peter had a pagan father. They lived alone in a small flat. She had suffered agonising surgery to her feet at one time, and she was concerned about my arm.

Peter kept coughing. I asked about his back. He developed scoliosis (curvature of the spine) three to four months after birth, and so had been in progressive plasters since a baby.

I did not know at the time that Gail had been engulfed in blackness and was sorely oppressed for a few days prior to this particular outing. Gail explained that Peter was simply not interested in Jesus, try as she might to encourage him. She studied the Bible and took him to a Fellowship.

He was listening to our every word, leaning forward, elbows on the table, chin cupped in the palms of his hands. I will never forget his face. Those coal black eyes pierced mine.

He spoke directly, "I don't really understand Jesus."

I found myself replying to this six year old.

"That's because you are under a curse. Would you like me to explain about Jesus?"

"Yes, I would", he responded, I glanced at Gail, a tear was trickling down her face.

"Quick Ernest, get my Bible from the car."

Suddenly the surroundings of our table blurred into a mist, I could vaguely hear everyone scurrying and chattering.

Heaven knows how long we had been at that table!

Peter listened attentively to every word of my explanations and I led him in the prayer to be set free of an ancestral curse, confessing and repenting of the sins and iniquities of his forefathers known and unknown. He asked for forgiveness of their sins and received forgiveness in the name of Jesus. I wielded the sword of the Spirit and cut him free.

The very second I stopped speaking he looked into

my eyes and said, "Can Jesus heal my back? And my cough?"

I replied in the affirmative. Ernest laid hands on his back and he puffed out all the spirits of fear, infirmity, rejection, anger – a whole stream of them. He inhaled the Holy Spirit with a magnificent breath, and when he had finished, he gave me again that direct gaze and said brightly, "I would like to ask Jesus into my heart."

Well, Gail's hanky was quite wet and by this time Ernest and I both had tears running down our cheeks! I could sense a desire that they were wanting to clear our table, but that would have to wait. We were on His Majesty's service!! Gail, bless her, prayed for my arm, and told me that she felt that the Lord would use my injury to His glory.

Chapter 10

Suffer The Little Children To Come Unto Me

Gail was so delighted and knew I was writing a book of testimony and the story of the Clinic. This is her own testimony:

"Being a Spirit-filled Christian for the past five years, I've always known the working of the Holy Spirit in my life. During the three weeks leading up to Easter 1988 I was feeling particularly unhappy at home. I felt the Lord speaking to me about spending too much time at home with my son of six years. I promised myself I would spend some of the time coming up to Easter at Gomshall Mill, doing my Easter shopping. The Tuesday before Good Friday I set out with my little boy to do this shopping.

As I wandered around I found that there was very little left as most things seemed to be sold out. Not feeling happy about returning home I decided to stay for a while and have a cup of tea and scone in the Gomshall Mill Tea Room. My son, whilst we were drinking, was busy waving to someone who had caught his eye across the room. He then asked my permission if he could say, "Hello" to a lady across the cafe. As I turned round I saw a very friendly lady waving and asking if she could speak to him. Her face was radiant and shining. I gave my permission and watched him walk across. As he approached the lady he said immediately, "I'm not supposed to talk to strangers," The lady agreed but added that it was all right provided mum is around. As he

38

returned to me his trousers were not pulled far enough up to cover a plaster jacket he was wearing for a deformity in his spine. This began at the age of approximately three to four months. However the treatment didn't begin until he was nearly two. It involved what seemed like endless trips to hospital at Stanmore for plaster jackets and braces. The plaster jackets were plaster of Paris which went from his chest to his hips (like a vest).

We then began to leave the cafe. It was after paying and walking to the door that the lady my son had waved to handed me a card. It said "Pearl A. Coleman. Christian Clinic for Environmental Medicine," then the address and telephone number. The word "Christian" stood out on the card above all the writing. I asked her whether or not she was a Christian to which she answered, "Yes, born-again." So I explained that I was too. She then went on to ask whether my son was still in nappies. I said "No". However, we got chatting and she asked me if I would like her to pray with my son as he was quite a fearful child. I agreed and after leading him in a prayer against curses and delivering him of several demons he then asked quite boldly if Jesus could come into his heart. She prayed that the Holy Spirit would fill him, after she led Peter into prayer of committing his life to the Lord.

The change in my son was immediate. After chatting and me having a quiet weep we left. As my son jumped into the car he exclaimed, "Thank God for that, I'm free!"

The release in him left me dumbstruck. I wouldn't drive home, I drove to some close Christian friends to tell them everything. Pearl gave me some very encouraging scriptures which I read later and they really were a blessing. Also with Pearl was her close friend and prayer-partner Ernest who has a ministry for praying for peoples' backs. He began touching Peter's back and wondered why he felt drawn to it. The plaster felt hard under his hand and he asked what the jacket was. So I explained about the deformed curvature he began to pray for my son and prophesied that it would be a complete healing.

As the days and weeks went by my son had a terrific desire to read the Bible, which was coming from the Holy Spirit. We have a quiet time at bedtime to pray and read the Bible. Before I had had such battles to get him to pray and hear the Bible stories – now it is a real Holy Spirit-inspired desire.

More fell into place as time went on. The weeks before I went to the Mill and met Pearl were so dark and depressing I just hoped God was going to pull me through them. Things got better, but my son was a new creation. I also believe during the weeks before meeting Pearl I was under attack with Satan trying to lay me low so that I wouldn't go out. Praise the Lord, I did out of obedience and what a blessing!"

Gail also pointed out to me the difference in Peter's eyes. The solid coal blackness had gone and one could see all the striations and varying shades in the iris of much lighter coloured eyes. Other people noticed this too and commented that his eyes had changed.

The thing that astonishes me most of all in Gail's testimony is that she saw my face as radiant and shining. It is so encouraging that the power of the Holy Spirit can penetrate such pain and despair.

One day a few weeks later, after my surgery, Gail brought Peter over to the Clinic. I could see that there was more to be done. I found out then that Gail was a mixture of Jamaican, Asian and English.

They had returned on a Clinic afternoon prior to when Peter was to visit the specialist. There were quite a few of us present including a local Pastor who had been extremely kind to me in the absence of my not having found a new Church since Liberty Christian Fellowship closed.

Whilst we were praying one of my staff said that she saw in the Spirit leather padded paws just like those of a monkey. Gail gasped! She told us that constantly she had to tell Peter to stand up and walk on two feet because he lolloped about like a monkey on all fours, not crawling on hands and knees but walking on hands and feet as monkeys do.

This was my first monkey spirit! So I called it out in the name of Jesus. The manifestation was astonishing. Peter immediately went down on all fours and climbed over everything with a gait that was typically apish. This went on for some time and the spirit did not want to leave. It was no childish crawling, but like a monkey springing from place to place and his form was swift and agile. I think monkeys are almost graceful in their movements.

When we were praying the Pastor saw Peter's back like two straight steel girders and said that he felt it was the Lord's promise that Peter's spine would ultimately be straight. This was confirmation of what Ernest had received from the Holy Spirit.

Just over two years later we met again. Gail had written a lovely note. She had purchased my first book and was excited about it. She filled me in with the details of past weeks as we all four had a reunion at the Old Mill.

We were met by a straight little boy with clear eyes carrying two bunches of flowers. One for Ernest, one for myself. The card read, 'To Pearl, thank you for everything. What would life be without you? Love from Gail and Peter (xx)'. Ernest had a similar card.

Gail told us how Peter now did not need any plasters and only a brace on week days. She said that the consultant had told her contrary to previous predictions that she now felt that this would not be permanent. Peter was looking great!

We had a lovely lunch. Peter still likes cake and sweet things. That will be the next step to get his diet right, to counteract the hyperactivity.

I laid hands on him afterwards in the car park and he received the gift of tongues.

41

Gail related to me an extraordinary thing. Her Jamaican mother was told by a doctor in Jamaica, "You have monkey blood."

Her mother was Rhesus Positive. One wonders if that let in a spirit which transferred from her daughter Gail to Peter. I will be describing the incredible story of a proven monkey spirit later in this book. The Rhesus monkey as most readers will know is a genus of pale brown Indian Monkey, commonly used in medical research.

Chapter 11

Lead Us Not Into Temptation

I have looked back in absolute amazement at both the revelations I received during my painful indisposition, and at the mighty work of refinement which was being wrought in me by my Father in heaven.

Because of my testimony against the use of homoeopathy in my last book I have been inundated with letters concerning its use, mainly from Christians who like myself, saw it as the answer to resistance of treatment with orthodox drugs.

Many have been grateful letters saying that reading my book finally nailed suspicions and feelings of dis-ease going on in their own minds concerning homoeopathic medicine. There have been a few cynical and abusive comments and some incredulity, but people's reactions are of course unimportant, as compared with my obedience. (Ezekiel 3:18-19, 33:6).

If anyone imagines that whilst in bed immobilized and in pain following my accident I did not turn over and over again in my mind the possibility of healing the pain and nerve damage of my injury with homoeopathic remedies, they would be wrong. Yes indeed, Satan tempted me frequently and persistently. Thank God that His word is true. (1 Corinthians 10:13) *There hath no temptation taken you but such as is common to man: but God is faithful, who will not suffer you to be tempted above that ye are able; but will with the temptation also make a way to escape, that ye may be able to bear it!*

43

My way to escape came in the form of a person actually bringing these remedies to my bedside. Ruth, whom I mentioned in Chapter 25 of "Go and Do Likewise", was coming to bath me, bless her. She had been such a faithful sister in Christ and was very special to me. I felt almost out of my mind prior to her arrival. I was withdrawing from an opiate prescribed for me, which I simply could not tolerate because of the side effects of nausea and vertigo. It did indeed dull the pain but caused me to retch. I was not actually sick but the whole of my body was traumatised at frequent intervals by non-productive retching. It is very fortunate that at this time I did not know what was actually wrong with my bones, for them to have shattered in that way.

Ruth rang me before leaving to ask if she should bring anything. I enquired if she still had her mini homoeopathic pharmacy. Replying in the affirmative she told me that although she had not used a single remedy since I received the revelation, she had not been convicted to actually throw the remedies away. She had quite a collection and had used a lot in the past for herself, friends and family.

The devil was working overtime on me. I asked her if she had any arnica, ruta graveolens, and symphatum (Knit-bone). She said she had all these and would bring them along. She did not think God would condemn me if I was in agony. Even as I was asking her these things, I somehow knew I would not dare to take them. I actually felt that I might die if I did, struck down for disobedience. There was also a part of me at that time which would have welcomed death as a relief, for not only was I harbouring a spirit of pain, I was still riddled with grief and mourning for a lost love. Praise God that as I write this book in 1990 I can state that I was once and for all set free of that grief a few months later in 1988 – and I have never looked back. Praise His name for evermore!

I believe that, not yet aware of the reason God could not protect me from the injury, I was still resentful and to some extent blaming Him. Yes, I was challenging my

Father like a hurt child.

Ruth gave me a luxurious bath and escorted me back to bed. Seated beside me with her Bible on her lap she produced the remedies I had asked for and placed them on it. I commented that I was grateful that she did not condemn me for asking her to bring them and told her that I wasn't really sure I dare swallow them anyway.

I could see that she was thinking deeply, when she said, and I think it was for herself as much as for me, "We need to pray about this. I want to get before the Lord and see what the Holy Spirit reveals."

So we prayed together in the Spirit having declared Matthew 10:26 *for there is nothing covered, that shall not be revealed: and hid, that shall not be known.* The small phials of pillules were on Ruth's open Bible as we prayed. My hand was on my Bible which I had opened at random.

At the very moment that Ruth screamed and flung the phials across my bedroom I was given by the Lord the scripture Ecclesiastes 10:1. I let Ruth speak first, her eyes were wide with horror.

She said, "As I prayed I saw your head very clearly. Over your head were hundreds of small serpents. As I prayed on I felt to open my eyes and regard the phials. As I did I saw a Cobra coiling around each bottle. I am going home to destroy my collection of remedies. Ugh! I can't wait!"

The Holy Spirit had convinced Ruth. Indeed whilst we were praying I was also convicted that tissue salts of 6x potency which masquerade under the description of biochemic remedies were also occult, so those too had to go from the Clinic pharmacy.

Also the Holy Spirit led me to a lifelong collection of wine and liqueur bottles of all shapes, sizes and colours, which decorated a pine shelf covering four walls of my pine kitchen. As a non drinker it may have seemed odd for me to have such a collection, but I always thought the bottles very attractive in shape and line. Especially I liked those of green and brown glass which looked good against the pine planks. Amongst them were some very rare and old bottles, but Ruth took them all to her dustbin. She told me as she piled them into a plastic sack that she had always had a check in her spirit with regard to these bottles and was glad to see them go. I felt that the Lord was saying, with the curse of alcohol in my blood line (although I have never fallen a victim to it), many of my relatives had and were still not free. My housing these alcohol containers could be binding them, even my own son.

It's a wonderful worldly saying for spiritual people. 'When in doubt, chuck it out!'

Before all this clearance took place, however, I shared with Ruth the scriptures the Lord had given me before she screamed.

I read from the King James Bible. Ecclesiastes 10 v. 1. "*Dead flies cause the ointment of the apothecary to send forth a stinking savour: so doth a little folly him that is in reputation for wisdom and honour.*" Well, the verse really astounded us. I certainly felt it was absolutely spot on. We then read it in the Amplified Bible. "*Dead flies cause the ointment of the perfumer to putrefy* (and) *send forth a vile odour: so does a little folly* (in him who is valued for wisdom) *outweigh wisdom and honour.*"

I got Ruth to get John Linden-Cook on my bedside telephone and shared with him, reading from the Amplified as it was still open.

He told me to look at verse 8 in that edition. "*He who digs a pit* (for others) *will fall into it, and whoever breaks through a fence or a stone wall, a serpent will bite him.*"

He also pointed out the first part of v. 11. "*If the serpent bites before it is charmed, then it is no use to call a charmer.*"

That scripture spoke to me so clearly, that had I disobeyed in spite of all the revelations the Lord had given, the wages of that sin would have been death!

Tough, but God does not compromise on unrepentance. He demands total obedience and if you think he's a wishy-washy woolly Father read the last verses of Isaiah 48, 57 and 66. In 1990 I received a further confirmation from an outside source of a sister whose healing progressed when she stood against selling homoeopathic remedies in a health store.

I will let her tell her own story.

Chapter 12

Testimony Against Homoeopathy

Nobody could forget the miraculous healing of Cheril given in her testimony in Chapter 32 of my book "Go and Do Likewise", entitled "Word of Knowledge Heals Tracheotomy".

Cheril, as readers will know, was also miraculously delivered of a spirit of anorexia bulimia in 1986 at the Clinic, and has remained free to this day. She is also fruit from the vine in as much that she works hard for the Kingdom and is vigilant against the enemy, helping many to find Jesus and casting out demons in His name.

Having left the Clinic where she had been my efficient secretary she joined a new Fellowship in Buckinghamshire. We had a wonderful reunion on November 5th, 1990 when she gave me the following testimony in her own words.

"After joining a new Fellowship I was thrilled to hear that the Fellowship had recently bought the lease of a wholefood shop in the heart of the village. This shop was to be used as an outreach to the village and was conveniently situated opposite the Post Office at the end of a closed walkway off the village green. I had some knowledge of health food products having previously worked with Pearl at her Clinic. Pamela who worked at the shop was a member of the Fellowship. She felt that God was directing us to have the shop as an outreach when the previous owner wanted to sell.

The next Sunday in church Pam asked me, together

with a friend, if I would like to be a helper in the shop. I witnessed positively to do this but felt I needed to pray first and seek the Lord's will.

During the next week I felt I must find this shop, which I did. It was a Wednesday afternoon so I found it shut. However I peered through the window and fell in love with this tiny little shop packed with natural foods and vitamins. As I turned to come away my eye caught an advert on the window for homoeopathic remedies. My heart sank to my boots! I had received revelation that this was of the occult and I could not be part of it. How was I going to tell Pam? Who was I, a newcomer to the Fellowship to tell them anything? Full of sadness I went home to pray and share with my husband. "No, of course you can't work there," he said.

Not being a bold person by nature it took much courage and prayer for me to visit Pam in the shop. I loved her dearly so I asked if we could pray first. This we did and the Lord honoured it by enabling me to share my experience of working with Pearl and receiving personal revelation. My fears melted as she shared that she had experienced a dis-ease about it and my revelation had been another confirmation to her. She had witnessed her concern to the leader of the Fellowship who had partially agreed with her, but nothing had been done about it. The next Sunday I spoke to the leader (thinking he was in agreement) and was about to give him "Homoeopathy Investigated" by Tony Bainbridge. He immediately stopped me short and said "Nothing is to bring about disunity in the Fellowship and things are only done after full agreement".

I felt deflated and hurt. I knew I had to share the truth so I went to see another lady in the Fellowship and after sharing, lent her two books, Roy Livesey's "Understanding Deception", which includes Pearl's testimony and "Homoeopathy Investigated" by Tony Bainbridge. She subsequently wrote a letter to the leader basically saying "if by stocking and selling homoeopathic medicines, we are causing offence to the weaker brethren, or if we are providing a stumbling block to others then it would be biblically sound to phase them out and not to reorder in the future (1 Cor.: 8) and (1 Cor. 6:12). The leader then approached another member to write a full report on homoeopathy and herbal medicines. Again she agreed and she also emphasized the occult roots. A shop meeting was arranged. I met together with Pam and the friend and I fasted and prayed that there should be agreement about removal of the homoeopathic medicines. The enemy is always at the door however! Pam was the first to speak and I could not believe my ears when she did not make a stand, only that we did not sell a lot of it so perhaps it was a good idea to phase it out! Another member, who used it, saw nothing wrong in it and had even visited a factory to investigate and had not "witnessed any pendulum swinging"! Everyone laughed and I could feel the enemy at work. "How about you, Cheril?" the leader asked. I told my story and emphasized, despite the division in the Church on this issue, that we, as a Christian shop, should not be part of anything likely to cause offence. It was finally agreed that we should phase out the items and not reorder. I felt a partial victory but knew the battle was still on. The friend and I continued to pray that we would not have to sell any whilst we were serving in the shop. In fact I started buying them myself and throwing them away!

In our Bible group we decided to listen to a set of tapes on New Age recently given at Gold Hill Baptist Church by John Hollidge. Homoeopathy was mentioned and I spoke to John on the telephone. He said that the Church was divided on this and although they had explored the 'for' homoeopathy angle with an expert, the 'against' view had not yet taken place so, as yet, no final judgement had been made by the leadership. Our leader was then part of that leadership! This brought me more understanding on the situation.

Six weeks later I went with a friend to hear Jackie

Pullinger speak at Guildford. The Holy Spirit's presence was amazing and after she had spoken, shared and introduced her team, we just waited on the Lord. His love was very close to me and as I responded to that in my heart. I knew He was telling me I had to make a stand. I felt at peace and asked that He would give me the courage I would need. At that very moment, a young Chinese girl, a member of Jackie's team, stepped forward to me. My eyes were closed. I felt a hand place itself over my throat and heard gentle words of the Holy Spirit. The Lord's power swamped me and I fell back on my seat with such an overwhelming presence of God's love. This young girl had no possible knowledge about me or the fact that I had a hole in my neck. I had worn a tracheotomy tube in my throat for 19 years as a result of a car accident, and 9 years ago I had been miraculously healed. I no longer needed the tube but I still had a small hole in my neck, because medically the scar tissue around it in the natural, prevented it from closing completely. When I got home that night there was a definite narrowing of the hole. "Praise the Lord!"

To make a stand for the Lord is painful and needs a step of obedience. I loved working in the shop, witnessing about the love of God, listening to people's needs and sowing seeds for the Kingdom. Who was I to make a fuss? I prayed, put pen to paper and wrote to Pam, asking her to share my resignation with the shop committee at their meeting the following day. She phoned me on receipt and thanked me for all I had done in the shop and told me she understood my situation. Then in a note she said "however when the offending items are no longer in the shop we hope to have you back on the team; your enthusiasm and help was always valuable. P.S. Black dustbin liner at the ready."

In the post the very next day, prior to the shop meeting in the evening, a reply came from the Rev Jimmie Song. I had written to him several weeks previously about my situation and had forgotten about not receiving a reply.

In the letter he said:

"Dear Cheril,

Thank you for your letter. There is a very good book just published this year on the subject. You will find it particularly helpful for the range of things you might be involved with at the Wholefood shop. It is called "Healing at any price? The Hidden Dangers of Alternative Medicine" by Samuel Pfeifer, with foreword by Selwyn Hughes. It covers various branches of New Age Medicine, including acupuncture, homoeopathy and herbal medicine. You are quite right – homoeopathy has its roots in occultism. Some practitioners use the pendulum for diagnosis. This is occultic. Of course I do not expect Christians to be involved with homoeopathy in this way, but like the drug scene, soft drugs can lead to highly toxic drugs. You might be aware that many Christians use homoeopathy, but I think this is leaving the door ajar for other things. You may be interested that many things in this area can hinder and retard spiritual growth and the loss of Christian assurance. Since you ask for my opinion, I would persuade you to keep clear of New Age Medicine and holistic health, especially in a Christian shop. May the Lord guide you and give you wisdom.

Yours sincerely,

Jimmie Song."

This was final confirmation and I felt that the letter should be shared at the meeting. I don't think it was a tool of witness to them but I felt that the Lord had honoured my stand.

I now began to hear others in the Fellowship airing their concern, but no one had spoken out. Our Fellowship had arranged a barbecue "outreach" evening with a speaker just over a week later. On the morning of this event I received a phone call from Pam in the shop, asking me if I was busy because she had a large black bin liner bag in the middle of the shop floor if I would like to dispose of it. Praise the Lord! It was full of remedies, homoeopathic lotions and creams etc. I went immediately.

That morning I had received a cheque for delivering Yellow Pages. The Lord prompted me to cash it and give it to the shop to honour Pam's obedience. I picked up the large black bag and together with Pat, a faithful prayer partner throughout the battle, we destroyed it ALL. The barbecue that evening was a great success!

I was thrilled to be asked once more to help in the shop – this I have continued to do. The Lord has blessed the work there sowing seeds for the Kingdom."

Cheril comments in her letter several times that she is not very bold. I think that she sells herself short. During the many times we witnessed together, not only was she bold, but after I ministered to her to receive the gifts, she received the gift of vision and years later this is still being confirmed in the Clinic. Cheril has had much to make her feel fearful, but she is a living testimony to having overcome in the strength of the Lord Jesus! Praise His name! May he bless her abundantly above all that I can think and pray.

Chapter 13

The Curse And Release

During those dark days of my indisposition and unrelenting pain I was also missing healthy exercise, part of which comprised long walks in the beautiful Surrey countryside. The weather for England was tantalisingly superb. I observed it everywhere as we drove backwards and forwards, from hospital to fracture clinic, to physio and so on, in what was for me a nightmarish circle.

Everywhere was blossoming. Hawthorn, cherry, white thorn, – transformed every common roadside as though it were decked for a wedding. Fine sprays of lace-like cow parsley intermingled with golden celandines and lesser stitchwort garlanded every verge, beckoning me to get out and get walking. I was full of self-pity. I couldn't even tie up the laces of my walking boots!

One very spiritually gloomy day, when I called on the Lord for an explanation of all these events, Ernest suggested that we drove out to the Sheepleas at Shere and gently walk along a nice easy path. The fear of falling in me was having to be dealt with, as was the pain. I was breathing those two spirits out several times a day in faith to defeat the enemy.

Catkins danced, birds heralded the Spring with joy, new lambs frolicked on their spindly legs. I feasted my eyes on the glory of creation as we walked slowly to the old oak, where I wrote the poem given in the Spirit for my last book.

I felt to sit down yet again under this tree, where so often I communed with my Maker and prayed in the Holy Spirit. The scenery was so lush and resplendent in so many shades of green. It was all so new looking, so fresh and perfect. As I sat there I closed my eyes recalling a poem called Springtime I had written thirty years previously, a time when I was unaware of the Holy Spirit, but when I used most fervently to talk and pray to God. I whispered it under my breath. Ernest had wandered off to watch the lambs.

SPRINGTIME

The Chestnut trees are budding forth,
The parsley's blooming in the hedge,
The slender birches seem to cry
That sister spring is keeping pledge
Of rebirth here.

The friendly wind is kissing soft,
The grasses tender in earth's bed,
And dancing sunbeams shine so bright,
They sprinkle every path they tread
With glitter dust.

The river winds its silver thread
With colours stolen from the sky,
And catkins whisper to the birds
That dainty gnats are flitting by,
Comes summer soon.

The hawthorn green, is stretching forth
Her spikey branches to the world,
Whilst velvet petals of the rose,
Are tightly still in sepals curled,
Not waking yet.

White garlands deck the orchard boughs,
Where snowflakes clustered in the cold
And peeping, blinking in the grass
Are daisies, with their yellow gold
Eyes, whitely frilled.

The fragrance of the violet, fills
The shaded woodland and the dell
With wondrous perfume, sweet and rare,
Which rises as the breezes swell,
Then gently fades.

And ever could I wander here,
Where nature's voices call to me,
Where chanting songsters echo now
The glory, o'er each greenwood tree.
God's music this.

I went immediately into the Spirit following the last verse.
As I prayed I got stronger, the sun was burning my face.
With my eyes no longer gazing at the surroundings I felt
myself really coming into the Lord's presence. I was
praying from my gut. I was calling out in that heavenly
language. "Father! Why did you let this happen to me,
your daughter whom you love so much? I know you love
me. Why did you not protect me?" I seemed to be aware
of Ernest sitting beside me also praying in the Spirit. I
was praying through a blackness for a very long time.
Suddenly I screamed out very loudly. I had heard the
words so clearly in my ears. "My daughter, I could not
protect you. You cursed your arms." I opened my eyes.
I turned towards Ernest, my pal. "Ernest, I did, I cursed
my arms. God just told me I cursed my arms. I did often,
I used to say to my dressmaker when she queried why I
wanted long sleeves in the summer. "Oh! I hate my arms,
they are so ugly." Helen always protested that she could
not see what I meant. I used to say to my masseuse
Barbara, "Can't you do anything about my ugly arms?"
Barbara was Polish. She used to laugh. "Ugly arms, it's
so ridiculous. You should see some of the arms I have to
cope with. There is nothing wrong with your arms."
    Beware of saying "I hate my legs, stomach, nose, hair
or anything," because you are putting a curse on what
God made. He made *all* of you, and you are hating what

He made. He saw all that He made *and it was good*. That includes any part of you that is not in your own eyes your most attractive feature. Don't curse that precious part of you. Do not separate it off from the rest. I have witnessed to so many patients on this matter and prayed for so many to break the self-imposed curse over them.

It's not as if I did not know better. I had done the same thing with my legs. I hated my legs as a child and said so. I would get dressed up for a party as a child in a pretty party frock, stand in front of the mirror, look at my legs, get undressed and go to bed.

What was wrong with my legs? Nothing really, but my eldest sister had legs like Betty Grable, which did not help me as a child. God made me like my earthly father, short in the limbs but powerful.

Because I cursed my legs they began aching, then throbbing, then feeling so very heavy. They were always tired legs, so I pronounced that I hated them even more. I finished up having my legs manipulated under general anaesthetic, and having them in plaster casts. I had a session with elastic bandages and built up shoes. I went into this hospital and that hospital and got poisoned by various drugs for a pain the medical profession couldn't identify. Finally I ended up in a hospital research centre. They were just about to operate when I realized we had got absolutely nowhere in ten years investigations. I discharged myself and left on crutches. I believe God spoke to me then. I gradually came to live with my legs because they were healthy and supple as I took to walking, cycling and climbing. Not until I heard a tape by Derek Prince in which he described how his wife Ruth also did not like her legs and said so – and asked Derek to pray for them on their honeymoon because they always hurt, did I realize what I had done.

I confessed and repented before the Lord and I truly never gave my legs a second thought. But what did I do? I transferred my hatred of self, my ugly spirit to my arms. I ought to have known better!

Whatever else I was, I was supple. My arms were strong. They lifted logs, carried huge slabs of stone when I helped build a wall and patio, they wielded an axe or a garden fork like any man.

My former husband did not have the muscles in his upper arms that I did, although extremely fit, and he used to pull my leg about it, saying that I looked like a cross between a Russian discus thrower and an all-in wrestler. Then years later as my son was growing into manhood, my former husband used to tease me over much, and I grew fitter and very physically active working gardens and becoming almost a builder's labourer as we jointly renovated our lovely old beamed home.

As I tell people I am teaching deliverance to — watch out, teasing can become a spirit of torment. When someone tickles another person habitually until the person becomes agonized – it ceases to be funny and borders into the realm of fear. "*Fear hath torment.*" As it is written!

So I began to look at my healthy arms and consider them too heavily built. Then I took on board that they were not feminine. From there I came to dislike them, then to disguise them by keeping them covered. Soon I was into cursing them. "I hate my arms." Truly there was, as with my legs, absolutely nothing to complain about. Satan allowed me to magnify my arms until I was built like Atlas! If you only knew how many Christians have done similar things, with noses, with bosoms, with hands! Have you ever seen a person with constantly sits on their hands, or keeps them in pockets? You could be looking at a curse, a self-imposed curse.

I fell on my face before the Lord upon this hillside. The pain in my arm diminished by the pain of repentance. Would I never learn? I wept, I confessed and oh how I repented from deep within. God had never deserted me. He was always there, but I cancelled out His protection with a self-imposed curse.

"What beautiful arms I have, Ernest." I said as I got

up and we walked back to the car.

Sharing this with my staff of three girls on Monday at the Clinic brought them all to their knees, confessing and repenting about parts of their anatomy they had spoken out that they hated. How we learn from one another! Praise God that His mercies are new every morning.

This was a turning point in the saga of my injury. From the moment I accepted that my God had not deserted me, I was released in my spirit. I had learned an awesome lesson, and release was around the corner.

Day after day I sat in my car, now in the garage, some twelve weeks, praying in the Spirit trying to turn the steering wheel, release the hand brake, slide the seat back and change gear. My hand and wrist just would not function, but I pressed on. I needed to get to Church. As readers of my book "Go and do likewise" will recall I returned in January 1988 from Penang, to find the fellowship I attended closed down in favour of the Bible school. I had not time to find a new fellowship before I met with the accident.

Finally I decided I must try to get down to a nearby church at the end of the road without asking anyone to give me a lift. I was really resenting the loss of my independence. I disliked having to ask all the time for lifts.

I thought I could work out a way to reverse the car out of the garage by degrees, crossing my hand over my lap to the gear change on the left, reversing it out with one hand. I hoped that if I could back it out in a straight line, once moving, the drive being on a slope, the steering wheel might turn. For weeks I struggled to do this, failing miserably, because I could not grip the wheel, and my whole body was weak through lack of exercise. Then I thought perhaps I could, if I strengthened my right arm, be able to do both movements with it to turn the wheel.

Ultimately on one glorious Sunday morning (it was the Sunday after I was released from the self-imposed curse) I achieved this with super human effort. I drove in a sweat in third gear at about fifteen miles per hour down the empty road, traffic free, due to it being Sunday. With great difficulty I changed to third gear with the right hand and kept in third gear. I had been told that one day I may be able to drive an automatic.

In church, when the space came for someone to bring a Word or a prophecy, I'll never know what made me do it. I stood up and read Revelation 12:10-11 and sat down feeling rather embarrassed. I was really driving illegally so I made sure I was the last in the car park to make an awkward exit.

When the coast was clear I got into the car. Without even thinking, with my left hand I flung the car into reverse and backed out. I had been instantly healed! Praise His name!

What a noise I made, I sang, I danced, I drove myself out to lunch, I was so excited and tearful with the joy of the Lord my healer. The next morning I washed my hair, rubbing with both hands. My arm was still bowed and crooked and very grotesque and with a huge lump at the back of the bracelet area into the hand. There was no way I could wear a watch. But I could drive. Praise the Lord! And my arms were beautiful!

Chapter 14

He Makes
The Crooked Straight

The Lord had been speaking to me for a whole year prior to my accident about witchcraft in the Church. Initially I could not believe what I was hearing and I felt very unnerved by these revelations. It was a cause for much prayer. I had indeed all those years ago asked the Lord in particular for a ministry against witchcraft and freemasonry (the same thing), so why should I be amazed at what He was showing me? Again I really valued the many teaching tapes on this subject by Derek Prince, and his honesty and fearlessness in stating his case. The deception of the elect surrounding these antics of Satan is truly disquieting and, certainly, the gift of the discerning of spirits is not something to desire if you wish to be all things to all men and entertain considerations other than having Jesus as Lord and Saviour!

The initial firsthand encounter I had with such witchcraft found me in a head-on confrontation with Satan. I had full opportunity to cut and run to be a man-pleaser, but I decided to stand whatever the cost. The results were extremely painful and left me feeling very battered and yet with a quiet peace which comes only from obedience.

I called out to God mightily during this horrific episode – even at one point longing almost to be told I was wrong.

At a particular stage in this dreadful experience I was involved in intercession for the Church concerned – crying out in despair at the deception.

"Give me a sign, Lord," I shouted with a very loud voice from the silence of my closet.

Suddenly I felt my injured arm moving, bones and muscles, and it just straightened out in front of my very eyes.

Later I got myself on the floor, on my stomach, putting my palms at shoulder level down on the carpet. Slowly I raised myself up holding my body level. My head was thudding, I was so excited. My arms were even, I could raise myself up in this way for the first time. Praise His lovely name!

I then took a long mirror off the wall, standing it on the floor leaning against the wall, repeating the exercise and watching myself come up slowly with both arms equally extended. My arms looked and felt the same. It was really true. He *does* make the crooked straight. It says so many times in the Holy Bible.

I had prayed those scriptures from Isaiah over myself for over a year when this happened. The one I liked most was Isaiah 42:16, "*And I will bring the blind by a way that they knew not; I will lead them in paths that they have not known: I will make darkness light before them, and crooked things straight. These things will I do unto them, and not forsake them.*"

The Lord did not indeed forsake me and when I met with the same situation of witchcraft in another Church it was most graciously received, the Lord honoured it, and I received the greatest blessing of all my experiences to date. None of these events came to pass until I had yet another shock to my system.

I could not restrain from a real curiosity about the nature of my injury. Why had such a slight fall caused such dreadful damage? There was my natural mind, my experience as a medical journalist nudging me into enquiry – and this curiosity increased because of the avoidance of my questions by specialists.

I must always have the truth at all costs!

I must have some sort of bone disease for my bones to have crumbled so easily. Time and again I was foisted off by the profession. Thus I decided to re-don my medical journalist's hat and attend a conference on bone disease at the Royal Society of Medicine in London.

I listened intently to many lectures by these eminent specialists. I certainly did not meet the criteria of faulty diet, smoking, heavy alcohol intake, lack of exercise. I was not childless, I had not experienced any uterine or ovarian surgery or suffered any thyroid problems or steroid treatment. So Lord, what's going on?

The Lord answered my questions very swiftly indeed. He gave me Proverbs 17:22.

"A merry heart doeth good like medicine: but a broken spirit drieth the bones."

Spot on again Lord! I had my spirit constantly broken by my father as a child, and later by the two men in my life whom I loved and lost. I put up a good fight, but I did end up a totally broken woman. Full of grief and sorrow.

If bones are dried up they will certainly become brittle. Grief and mourning were spirits I had harboured for decades before deliverance. But too late, for the rot had set in my bones! I needed to replace that sorrow with joy to complete the work. The joy of the Lord is my strength (Nehemiah 8:10).

How was I to do that? In one word – obedience. Total and absolute obedience – for there is no other way for lasting joy and peace.

Whilst mulling all these revelations over in my mind and being peaceful in the Closet, which was the beginning of my complete yielding – although I did not know it at that moment of time, I was going through the business of medical investigations – which I had insisted upon, following the conference at the Royal Society of Medicine.

It was emphatically denied by my consultant that I could have osteoporosis but a bone scan revealed the shattering truth. Not only did I have it but I had it very badly indeed. I was told at one stage quite brutally that 95% of the population had better bones than I.

Even so, because I deplore ignorance and have never considered it bliss, it was better to be informed so that I could work out a plan and consult God, my maker!

Meanwhile I seemed to be surrounded by Christian friends in the profession, formerly against my having treatment with Hormone Replacement Therapy, suddenly advising me to get on it quickly. The side effects can be cancer or a stroke!

The pain in my hips was the thing which alarmed me most. I did not fancy a spontaneous fracture of the hip. People say "I fell and broke my hip!" but that is not the case, or rarely is. People with that disease fall because their hip snaps.

Again Satan had a field day, I could see the Clinic closed, no income, loss of my home, etc, etc. I was not at that time in my life really dependent on the Lord for my supply. The mortgage, the rates, the heating bills, the overheads had never been an easy matter for me as a single woman. It was about three years at the time, since I raised my fees and I certainly never intend to raise them again *whatever*. Accountants do not like this since everything else goes up – but the Lord does!

Prayer and fasting did not bring me a really positive answer to my dilemma. Nobody could get me a Word. A pastor from a local Church said he had a strong hunch I should go on it.

Then one of my team said she could not get a Word – but constantly had a story she had once heard put back into her mind. It was the story of the man drowning in the ocean calling out to Jesus to save him. A lifeboat came alongside as he struggled but the helpless man refused help and the lifeboat went away. He plunged into the depths of the sea again coming up for the last time calling "Jesus, save me!" Thereupon a helicopter hovered overhead and lowered a ladder. Again the drowning man refused, repeating that Jesus had promised to save him. He drowned and questioning the Lord in heaven about His promises to save him, he was told "Well, I sent a lifeboat and then a helicopter and you ignored both."

So that was that. I grabbed the lifeline. Dr Joy Seevaratnam, when I told him at Christmas 1989 when I returned to Penang, said that he thought it was wisdom, but he was not happy about it long term.

"You'll need to get a Rhema," he told me.

Part II

Teaching and More Testimonies

Chapter 15

Response to "Go And Do Likewise"

When my book "Go And Do Likewise" was published in June 1990 I had no idea that I would receive such a deluge of mail. I actually did not doubt that there was a great harvest of infirm, terrified, molested and agonized out there. What has really shaken me is the continued absence of teaching on the ministry of deliverance in so many Churches crammed with the lame.

My team and I have been busily ministering and counselling as many of these desperate victims as possible, but frankly we cannot cope with the deluge even though the team has been added to. Many persons who write in, sometimes eight foolscap pages with both sides covered in hardly decipherable descriptions of misery and heartbreak, believe, understandably, that they are the only person sending in such a letter!

I calculated in one week the actual reading time for letters was 40 hours! Others state apologetically that they expect I am overwhelmed with correspondence requesting help. There are heart cries of "If only I (or we) could get to you I feel certain you could help me (or our whole family)".

Numerous writers begin their desperate correspondence with the words "There is no doubt that God led me to your book". Those words have led me to challenge the Lord with "Well, Lord if you did lead them to my book, you must have had some notion that there was an answer for these folk in their plights. And I cannot cope Lord! HELP!"

One girl had seen her mother stabbed and strangled when she was 4 years old – and was facing meeting her father again. There were other letters involving murder, witnessed or unsuccessful attempts on their lives by their own mothers, not only with unsuccessful abortion but by strangulation and suffocation. These people all have to be set free of a spirit of murder and/or death which needs dealing with in Jesus' name.

There have been vile cases of torture, including sexual torture of hideous description, not to mention rape, incest, bestiality and such rejection and grief that I have had to stand fast against the enemy who would wear me down with the agony of it all.

In Israel this year at the Shavuot conference May 28th – June 2nd I heard it preached by Johannes Facius that, "Satan's first job is to wear out the saints." I can believe it!

I have been greatly blessed by those who have allowed the book to minister to them and set them free. I would like to share some of the fruit later.

I have indeed received tremendous encouragement by many pastors unknown to me and other Church elders, urging me to continue standing and to press on boldly. The one comment I treasured most was "It's tough stuff – but it's needed." There have been many prophecies sent to me for which I am also grateful, confirming past prophecies over my life, which had been squashed in the past by various Church leaders – leaving me often not a little confused.

There have been numerous requests for "What happened next?" "Tell us about your accident, your healing," — so many that I was convicted to write another book without delay. One almost feels obliged to respond to such a receptive readership! Many have asked how they can learn the ministry and requested to come to one of my condensed teach-ins on the subject of deliverance.

I have naturally prayed all this through at a time when the Lord is also requiring that I see prayer for Israel, for the peace of Jerusalem and the apple of His eye as an End-time priority. I and many others are needed to get our faces in the rug for Israel, to bind the strong man from usurping the sovereign will of God over that land. Visiting Israel for the first time in May 1990, I was not only afforded the privilege of ministry (totally unexpected) in Israel, but I was deeply moved and convicted that I had in my spiritual walk totally neglected the call on my life as an intercessor for the Jews. I had to fall on my face and confess and repent my disgraceful ignorance of God's commands in this respect. I can see already that obedience in this matter has brought great peace and reward.

I can honestly say that not a single Church in Britain ever taught me on End-time prophecy or of the need to pray for the peace of Jerusalem. Here I am again for the umpteenth time indebted to the teaching of Derek Prince Ministries.

So I have received in my spirit a conviction to set down my very simple biblical exposition of the ministry of deliverance received as a disciple (student) and taught in faith to those who attend our meetings.

There are many large tomes and manuals on deliverance ministry and this is not to be one such. It is a brief and simple outline, which many have followed and gone out to do likewise!

It is to encourage you to make a bold start in faith to set the captive, even yourself free. To minister to your families and friends in need, to recognize and to expel demons in the name of Jesus Christ, to understand your authority to do so and the function of our beloved teacher, the Holy Spirit, in all this.

I was taught by others, many with great, effective and proven ministries. I have badgered many I have never met, by post – and have always been met with such love and encouragement from mighty but oh so humble men and women of God.

Let humility be your watchword. Remember that His

grace is sufficient and invite the Holy Spirit to teach and reveal as you study the next chapters on this ministry.

Having told you in the previous chapter how my crooked arm was made straight, I then suffered the shock of discovering that I had severe osteoporosis. This obviously accounted for my bone injury being so devastating. The Lord then gave me ample opportunity to take my own medicine and yield to Him in yet other areas of my life, just when I thought that life had settled down!

Chapter 16

Introduction To Teaching On Ministry Of Deliverance

Before you begin this condensed teaching please invite the Holy Spirit to be your teacher and guide. Ask the Lord to reveal through His Spirit any areas of need for revelation in your life. Remember that the Holy Spirit is the Spirit of all truth, that He will lead you into all truth so that every hidden thing is revealed. (John 16:13). This simple teaching has enabled many to "Go And Do Likewise". There are many large books and manuals on this subject which are very complicated. This teaching is essentially for beginners, hungry to make a start. Ask the Father for wisdom, (James 1:15) but do not wait until you think you are absolutely perfect for the job! You never will be. Step out in faith! God is looking for people who are not lukewarm (Revelation 3:15), He will, I promise you honour every step you make to set the captive free, even if you make a few mistakes on the way. I made many! God is not finished with me yet – and if I ever get cosy about what I am learning He is swift to correct me and I am grateful for that (2 Timothy 3:16). 2 Timothy 2:15 says, "*Study to shew thyself approved unto God, a workman that needeth not to be ashamed, rightly dividing the Word of truth.*" Remind yourself of this *scripture daily*.

I am using the King James Bible for this teaching.

Mark 16: 15-18. "*And he said unto them, Go ye into all the world, and preach the gospel to every creature. He that believeth and is baptized shall be saved; but he that believeth not shall be damned. And these signs shall follow them that believe; In my name shall they cast out devils; they shall speak with new tongues; They shall take up serpents; and if they drink any deadly thing, it shall not hurt them; they shall lay hands on the sick, and they shall recover."*

Please note that the great commission is a command. GO is not an option. Note also that these were the last words of Jesus to the eleven Apostles before He ascended into heaven.

I am sure many of you will recall leaving notes for your family when you were going away. Invariably the last piece of the message you leave is the most important.

"And don't forget to feed the cat" or "Don't forget to leave the key out for me on my return" or "Don't forget to cancel the newspapers" etc., etc.

Clearly when we study the gospel we can see how important this last message from our Saviour was.

Look at Matthew 28:19-20. *"Go ye therefore, and teach all nations, baptizing them in the name of the Father, and of the Son, and of the Holy Ghost: Teaching them to observe all things whatsoever I have commanded you: and, lo, I am with you alway, even unto the end of the world. Amen."*

I have believed that the teaching I have done at the Clinic on the subject has been in obedience to do what the Bible instructs. I haven't had any special training, I am a complete nobody, but God has honoured my attempts because He knows my heart. If you feel feeble, let me tell you I always feel feeble and that I am falling far short of what God would like. I comfort myself with the words, *"When I am weak, then am I strong"* (2 Corinthians 12:10).

So that is why we should desire to operate in the gift of the discernment of spirits. One cannot cast a demon out of a captive unless one has discerned it through that gift. It is not a guessing game or a soulish activity.

There is also a need to take authority in our families in times of distress and sickness, or any other need. We need to know how to rebuke a fever in a sick child, for example, or cast out a spirit of fear in a child fearful of attending school because of bullying.

We have the authority given in Matthew 18:18 to bind and to loose.

"Verily I say unto you, Whatsoever ye shall bind on earth shall be bound in heaven: and whatsoever ye shall loose on earth shall be loosed in heaven."

If you were attending a football match, when there was a stampede, due to the transference of a spirit of fear from one spectator to another, resulting in the horrors we witnessed on our television screens in recent years, you would need to act quickly.

Likewise you may recall the terrible fire at King's Cross tube station, the agonizing horror for those engulfed by smoke who found their escape routes blocked by closed iron gates. One can speak to these mountains in the name of Jesus. (Mark 11:23). *"For verily I say unto you, That whosoever shall say unto this mountain, Be thou removed, and be thou cast into the sea; and shall not doubt in his heart, but shall believe that those things which he saith shall come to pass, he shall have whatsoever he saith."*

Faced with rot in a main supporting beam at the rear loggia of the Clinic, with a builder jabbing the beam all along with a Stanley knife to show me how the powdered wood poured out like fine silk, I restrained him from further jabbings. As he gabbled on about the beam tying in with a supporting roof structure I said,

"Stop. I refuse it in Jesus' name. I'll get the girls to pray in agreement."

When the staff arrived for work the next day, four of us laid hands on the beam in faith. I cursed the rot and commanded it to be confined to that one beam. When later the builder came to hack it away, he could give absolutely no explanation why the rot suddenly cut off and was indeed confined to a single beam. Of course he didn't know my Father.

74

My mother, now eighty years, had a terrible fear of falling two years ago.

I prayed with her, the fear was cast out and that was that. Similarly I have dealt with many of her worries. Elderly ladies do often fear losing things, being burgled and being ill when they are alone. My mother, praise God, has lost those fears through prayer. She asks the Holy Spirit where things are!

Many years ago, John Linden-Cook wanted to build an extension to his home. The foundations were deep but kept filling with water. A land drain ran across council property and, although this was cleared, the water persisted. The council finally said that unless the water went then building could not proceed; all this despite a mass of legal correspondence.

Arriving home after a Gospel meeting, John felt led to take authority over this situation. Standing over the hole by the back door John commanded the water to go and not return in the name of Jesus, and then went to bed. The next morning he went down and the water had gone – the building was duly completed. All thanks be to the Lord Jesus.

I repeat such experiences of myself and others to encourage you. Dr Joy Seevaratnam actually prayed in faith for two seats on a plane which were not available, and for two air tickets to materialize in a drawer in the airport. He got both! Praise the Lord!

AUTHORITY

Read all of Luke 10 especially Luke 10: 1-2. "*After these things the Lord appointed other seventy also, and sent them two and two before his face into every city and place, whither he himself would come. Therefore said he unto them, The harvest truly is great, but the labourers are few: pray ye therefore the Lord of the harvest, that he would send forth labourers into his harvest.*" Also, Luke 10: 16-20 "*He that heareth you heareth me; and he that despiseth you despiseth me; and he that despiseth me despiseth him that sent me. And the seventy returned again with joy, saying, Lord, even the devils are subject unto us through thy name. And he said unto them, I beheld Satan as lightning fall from heaven. Behold, I give unto you power to tread on serpents and scorpions, and over all the power of the enemy; and nothing shall by any means hurt you. Notwithstanding in this rejoice not, that the spirits are subject unto you; but rather rejoice, because your names are written in heaven."*

Please note however in verse 17 that DEVILS should read DEMONS. Make a note in the margin of your Bibles. There is only one DEVIL, singular (Satan, Lucifer, the son of perdition, etc.), but demons or spirits are plural – they are many.

The word disciple actually means student. To be a student you must be a disciplined studier of the Word of God, the Holy Bible as we are exhorted in 2 Timothy 2:15. You will note as you study that the Bible is full of "hearkens". To hearken is to listen and to obey. James 1:22 states quite clearly – *"but be ye doers of the Word, and not hearers only, deceiving your own selves."*

It is absolutely fruitless, and I use that word advisedly, to read, to listen, to hear, but not to obey. If we instruct our children, we expect obedience. If we say to our little child:

"When you've finished playing with your cycle, put it away in the shed," we don't expect to find the cycle left under the front porch. So it is with our heavenly Father instructing us His children.

So if you can agree with me that the command to cast out demons came from our Lord after all He endured on the cross and before He ascended into heaven, that those were indeed His last minute instructions, then we can proceed.

Please note also that in the Lord's commission casting out demons is presented before laying hands on the sick so that they shall recover.

How often have you in your Christian experience seen

as I have, the same dear brothers and sisters going up front week after week for prayer concerning their illnesses and they are forlorn because nothing seems to be happening. This is because quite often the spirit of fear or the spirit of infirmity needs casting out in Jesus' name. I've sat in churches with a gag and invisible handcuffs on in frustration as I have watched this constant non event. People do get fearful when, for all the prayer that goes on for them, they still remain sick. I have found in the Clinic that fear is a root spirit in the cause of M.E. (Myalgia Encephalitis). People are terrified that they will never get well, because the medical profession does not have the answer. But Jesus does! I speak from personal experience, I was healed of M.E. I give him all the glory for that. Others have also been healed of M.E. at the Clinic.

Chapter 17

Reluctance To Minister In Deliverance

There are two main reasons why people shy away from deliverance ministry. The first reason is fear. Yet we know, for it is written, that *"God hath not given us the spirit of fear; but of power, and of love and of a sound mind."* (2 Timothy 1:7). There is also a spirit of the fear of man in so many Christians, which alas displaces the spirit of the fear of the Lord. We have to reverse that state of affairs.

Psalm 110:10 reads, *"The fear of the Lord is the beginning of wisdom: a good understanding have all they that do his commandments: His praise endureth for ever."*

The second reason people steer clear of obedience to this portion of the great commission is because they do not want to feel or appear foolish.

1 Corinthians 3:18-19. *"Let no man deceive himself. If any man among you seemeth to be wise in this world, let him become a fool, that he may be wise. For the wisdom of this world is foolishness with God. For it is written, He taketh the wise in their own craftiness."*

1 Corinthians 1:27. *"But God hath chosen the foolish things of the world to confound the wise; and God hath chosen the weak things of the world to confound the things which are mighty."*

You must be ready to be a fool for Jesus. This means that the sin of pride must be dealt with in all our lives. If we consider that we do not have pride then we very likely have a spirit of deception or self-deception.

There are many spirits of pride. Big pride, little pride,

false pride, spiritual pride (found in many Churches). The monarch of all pride is the Leviathan spirit, referred to in the Amplified Version of the Bible as the crocodile spirit (Job 41 Amp.). Readers would do well to study that chapter, it is quite a revelation on pride.

In his comprehensive handbook of lists of demons entitled "Deliverance, the Children's bread", Robert A. Ellender lists the demons experienced in ministry under the heading of pride as follows.

PRIDE

Arrogant pride; pride in self; spiritual pride; physical pride; intellectual pride; social status pride; humble pride; pride of life; occult pride; sexual pride; mental pride; professional pride; stubborn pride; false pride; vain glory; prancing; attention getter; praise honour & glory; superiority; self righteousness; conceit; self exaltation; Leviathan; (a very strong spirit of pride; see more information under religious spirits) little pride; (everybody needs me) vanity; self attention; love of recognition; high imagination; self reliance; self sufficiency; self conceit; unwillingness to bend.

That is quite a formidable list! Have you any of these? I had quite a lot to be dealt with. For myself they came out when the spirit of deception was dealt with over homoeopathy, aspects of the faith, and the prosperity message and freemasonry. Deception or self-deception can block the exit of spirits of pride. If you think you do not have pride you could be deceiving yourself. We have to be brutally honest. I had great pride in being self-reliant and self-sufficient. I learned a mighty lesson learning to rely only on God. What a freedom that is. I recommend it.

Should you wish to obtain Robert Ellender's excellent handbook it is currently $4 plus postage from Harvest Christian Fellowship, N108 W17376, Lilac Lane, Germantown, Wisconsin 53022, USA.

Chapter 18

Ten Necessities For Ministry

These necessities are absolute. They are golden rules.
1. Motivation.
2. Agreement between ministry team members.
3. Agreement between team and person seeking ministry of deliverance.
4. Never force deliverance on anyone. (*Exceptions see below)
5. There must be no hostility between the team and the person seeking deliverance. If hostility occurs as demons are being told to go, that is no problem. It is not the person who dislikes you or is hostile, but what is being commanded to leave them in Jesus' name.
6. People must therefore request deliverance and respect you.
7. Humility. (2 Chronicles 7:14-15)
8. Confession.
9. Repentance – Godly heart repentance, not just repentance uttered with the mouth.
10. Forgiveness. This is not only forgiving those who have hurt you but self forgiveness.

Unforgiveness
Derek Prince teaches that we should forgive others in enlightened self-interest. Some people really struggle and call out that there are certain people they cannot forgive.

This has been my frequent experience, especially in cases of betrayal or incest, which of course is also betrayal as well as molestation. Those who have been humiliated frequently are resistant to forgiving their tormentors. If real difficulty persists I lead those I am praying for in a prayer as follows.

"Dear Jesus, I know in the Holy Bible you say that first we must forgive others, and I am finding this so difficult to do. I really cannot do it in my own strength, so I do it in your strength, Jesus, because the Bible says I can do all things through Christ Jesus, who strengthens me. (Philippians 4:13). So in your strength, Jesus, I do now unconditionally forgive" – then get the person to name the individual or individuals to forgive and bless them.

I remember one dear sister who wept bitterly because she could not forgive her stepmother humiliating her. You need to be unshockable about the cruelty human beings inflict on each other, especially the weak and defenceless.

Only hours of closet prayer and time alone with the Holy Spirit can equip you to bear the burdens of others. A scripture I have often given to my team is one that the Lord gave me early in this ministry, Romans 15:1.

"We then that are strong ought to bear the infirmities of the weak, and not to please ourselves."

Focus

This must be on Jesus and only Jesus, keep your eyes on Jesus. Pearl Coleman has never cast out a demon in her life, or healed anyone. We all must remember we are humble instruments of His calling. The love of Jesus must be evident in the team, and that love of Jesus in them must be for each other and those being ministered to. The anointing of the Holy Spirit is essential. If it is not there you will be wasting your time. He is a gentleman who only comes by invitation. He comes that Jesus and only Jesus is glorified.

Team Ministry

When team ministry follows teaching from the Word to a gathering, or at a pre-arranged deliverance with the team in attendance, we always enter His courts with praise and thanksgiving. We speak out Psalm 91, the psalm of God's sure protection and put on the whole armour of God. (Ephesians 6:14-17). Holy Communion is celebrated, followed by the Lord's prayer. Then we speak out the blood scriptures from cards graciously supplied by Derek Prince Ministries as follows:

By This I Overcome The Devil

Revelation 12:11 –

They (the believers on earth) *overcame him* (Satan) *by the blood of the Lamb* (Jesus Christ), *and by the word of their testimony.* (That is, they testified to what the Word of God says about the blood of Jesus).

Ephesians 1:7 –

In whom we have redemption through his blood, the forgiveness of sins, according to the riches of his grace.

Psalm 107:2 –

Let the redeemed of the Lord say so, whom he hath redeemed from the hand of the enemy.

1 John 1:7 –

But if we walk in the light, as he is in the light, we have fellowship one with another, and the blood of Jesus Christ his Son cleanseth us from all sin.

Romans 5:9 –

Much more then, now justified by his blood, we shall be saved from wrath through him.

Hebrews 13:12 –

Wherefore Jesus also, that he might sanctify the people with his own blood, suffered without the gate.

1 Corinthians 6:19-20 –

What? Know ye not that your body is the temple of the Holy Ghost, which is in you, which ye have of God, and ye are not your own? For ye are bought with a price: therefore glorify God in your body, and in your spirit, which are God's.

I testify to Satan personally as to what the Word says the blood does for me. Through the blood of Jesus I am redeemed out of the hand of the devil.

Through the blood of Jesus all my sins are forgiven.

The blood of Jesus Christ, God's Son, continually cleanses me from all sin. Through the blood of Jesus I am justified, made righteous, just-as-if-I'd never sinned. Through the blood of Jesus I am sanctified, made holy, set apart to God.

My body is a temple of the Holy Spirit, redeemed, cleansed by the blood of Jesus. Satan has no place in me, no power over me, through the blood of Jesus.

This confession is taken from audio teaching by Derek Prince from the Derek Prince Ministries, P.O. Box 169, Enfield, EN3 6PL, United Kingdom.

I was delighted to find in Penang, West Malaysia, the Full Gospel Assembly of Penang have their vast congregation regularly speak out these scriptures.

Of course all this is not possible during Clinic time when I may have to quickly deal with something bothering a patient. Then I simply call a couple of my staff up both to catch if need be and as a witness. That is why it is so necessary to be prayed up and walking in the Spirit.

*Exceptions to ministry without permission.

e.g. If someone presents suddenly with an epileptic fit. If someone lunges at you with a knife – bind that spirit of murder quickly. If someone is laying dying at the scene of a road accident call out that spirit of death in Jesus' name. Ministry to sick infants in their cots or beds, etc.

Chapter 19

Reliance on the Holy Spirit

Reliance on the Holy Spirit must be absolute.
John 16: 12-15

12 *I have yet many things to say unto you, but ye cannot bear them now.*

13 *Howbeit when he, the Spirit of truth, is come, he will guide you into all truth: for he shall not speak of himself; but whatsoever he shall hear, that shall he speak: and he will shew you things to come.*

14 *He shall glorify me: for he shall receive of mine, and shall shew it unto you.*

15 *All things that the Father hath are mine: therefore said I, that he shall take of mine, and shall shew it unto you.*

The Holy Spirit will only come if the ministry is to glorify Jesus. Keep your eyes on Jesus and not upon the instrument of deliverance. By all means support the person ministering with gentle Holy Spirit utterance. The whole meeting must be led by the Spirit. Romans 8:14 *"For as many as are led by the spirit of God, they are the sons of God."* You come as babes and mature as sons. The Holy Spirit is a person — not an impersonal influence, not a system, not half a sentence in the Apostle's creed, not theological. The Holy Spirit, like Jesus, is Lord! The Lordship of Jesus is over the Church. The Lordship of the Holy Spirit is in the Church. Two tapes which set this teaching out so well are:

How to be led by the Spirit. Nos. 134 and 135 and
Continually led by the Holy Spirit No. 14137.

Derek Prince Ministries, P.O. Box 169, Enfield, EN3 6PL or P.O. Box 3000, Ft. Lauderdale, FL 33302. USA.

I have learned so much by playing these tapes over and over again. I believe in repetition. That's how we learned our tables years ago and personally I do not feel that any new fangled method of learning has ever exceeded the thoroughness of repetition. I recall the absolute delight in a traffic jam one day needing to speak out the blood scriptures – only to find that I knew them off by heart. Remember too – always ask the Holy Spirit to teach you. He is an excellent tutor.

The primary requirement for developing a relationship with the Holy Spirit is sensitivity. It is the absolute and vital qualification for which there is no substitute whatsoever. Cultivate that sensitivity as you would a delicate young plant and nurture it with love.

The Holy Spirit is characterized by the dove. The dove is an extremely alert and timid bird which scares easily. The kind of person the Holy Spirit desires to relate to is gentle and sensitive. Submission to the Father and the Son is simply not possible unless we recognize and understand the Holy Spirit's Lordship. The Holy Spirit is characterized by the dove. Jesus Christ is characterized by the lamb.

John 1:29-32

29 *The next day John seeth Jesus coming unto him, and saith, Behold the Lamb of God, which taketh away the sin of the world.*
30 *This is he of whom I said, After me cometh a man which is preferred before me: for he was before me.*
31 *And I knew him not: but that he should be made manifest to Israel, therefore am I come baptising with water.*
32 *And John bare record, saying, I saw the Spirit descending, from heaven like a dove, and it abode upon him.*

The lamb characterises purity, meekness and sacrifice.

The Holy Spirit desires the glorification of Jesus, He looks for the Lamb nature. That is not pride, arrogance, aggression or criticism. He's looking for the life laid down. The life laid down is servanthood. In John 1:32 we read that the Holy Spirit (the dove) descended upon Jesus and remained. The Lamb nature is very attractive to the dove.

Jesus' entire ministry was based on one thing only, the anointing.

Remember that Jesus took the scroll of Isaiah (Luke 4:17-19) *"And there was delivered unto him the book of the prophet Isaiah. And when he had opened the book, he found the place where it was written, the Spirit of the Lord is upon me, because he hath anointed me to preach the gospel to the poor; he hath sent me to heal the brokenhearted, to preach deliverance to the captives, and recovering of sight to the blind, to set at liberty them that are bruised, to preach the acceptable year of the Lord."* Speak out these words as you receive the anointing which breaks the yoke. Jesus is the one who baptises with the Holy Spirit.

Fasting

This is a personal recommendation. For serious deliverance and, yes, all deliverance ministry is serious, but I mean in cases where protracted ineffective prayer and healing has been given to a person over a long while, where murder, abortion, or the occult are involved. Or in ministry which is to follow a teaching such as this, where the Word has gone forth – a three day fast is a real blessing to those ministering. It not only leaves one sharper in the gift of the discerning of spirits, the physical body becomes energized to continue in ministry for many hours without carnal wrestlings!

A fast should be proclaimed. (Joel 1:14) and sanctified. Matthew 6:17 instructs us to anoint our heads and wash our faces. I always do this.

Fasting puts you into a position to hear from God.

When we do fast we learn rapidly how carnal we are and what a priority of time eating has over our lives.

We see in 2 Chronicles 20 when Jehoshaphat was in great fear with the people, that he sets himself to seek the Lord proclaiming a fast throughout all Judah, verse 3. The Spirit of the Lord responded to the obedience of that vast gathering and instructions were given (verse 15-17) which were obeyed and victory followed in a mighty manner.

Men's bellies not infrequently dominate their lives. People are governed by the time of their next meal. Alas, we see this in the Church. People get home late for Sunday lunch because the preacher has overstepped the time allowed for the sermon and they have roast pastor for lunch!

In Acts 13:1-2 prophets and teachers were gathered together. Paul was not an Apostle at this time. As they ministered to the Lord and fasted the Holy Spirit spoke to them and said *"separate me Barnabas and Saul"*. Saul was of course Paul. In that atmosphere of prayer and fasting the Holy Spirit said something which changed the world. Paul and Barnabas became Apostles and that assignment brought into being two thirds of the New Testament.

In Matthew 6:16 we are clearly told not to walk around with downcast faces, to show off that we are fasting. The reward should come from God only who knows our secret, that we are fasting. Of course if there is agreement for many to fast it is no secret between those involved. But if you will excuse the pun, don't make a meal of it! Keep yourself clean and spruce, believe for the reward of fasting, not for the punishment of an empty stomach! Be careful not to make fasting a religion. Do not be tempted to draw sympathy or praise from people. The temptation to fall into spiritual pride will be there.

A tip for fasting is that abstinence from tea and coffee a week before a fast will cut out headaches.

Fasting is a subject which could take pages and many

excellent teachings on this subject are available from Derek Prince Ministries, P.O. Box 169, Enfield EN3 6PL. "Shaping History Through Prayer and Fasting" is an excellent book.

Chapter 20

Activity and Nature of Demons

What Demons Do

Firstly demons recognise you. Mark 1:23-27

23 *And there was in their synagogue a man with an unclean spirit; and he cried out,*

24 *Saying, Let us alone; what have we to do with thee, thou Jesus of Nazareth? art thou come to destroy us? I know thee who thou art, the Holy One of God.*

25 *And Jesus rebuked him, saying, Hold thy peace, and come out of him.*

26 *And when the unclean spirit had torn him, and cried with a loud voice, he came out of him.*

27 *And they were all amazed, insomuch that they questioned among themselves, saying, What thing is this? what new doctrine is this? for with authority commandeth he even the unclean spirits, and they do obey him.*

Demons will recognise you, they know exactly who you are and of course they will dislike you. They are immediately threatened by someone with the gift of the discerning of spirits, and may put up a show of hostility in the person in which they reside, attempting to cause you to back off. This is where you need to know scriptures which declare your authority over demons. e.g. 1 John 4:4: *Greater is he that is in you than he that is in the world.*

2 Corinthians 10:4: *For the weapons of our warfare are not carnal, but mighty through God to the pulling*

down of strong holds.

So, Jesus' reputation began, his fame spread abroad (Mark 1:28) and people were very impressed. They followed him, they went where the action was in their droves. And so it is today, people are tired of passive Churches. They want to see that *Jesus Christ is the same yesterday, today and forever* (Hebrews 13:8), that Jesus is indeed alive. Hallelujah!

We have to keep our eyes on Jesus who is 'the author and finisher of our faith.' Indeed this cannot be over-emphasised. But many devout Spirit-filled Christians will be seen flocking to wherever certain men or women preach on deliverance, healing and freedom from curses, not because they have got their eyes off Jesus, but because they have seen the action following the dynamic preaching of the Word and find it encouraging and inspiring.

I never saw an empty hall or Church where Derek Prince, Bill Subritzky or Dr. Joy Seevaratnam were preaching. Rather I saw people standing because there were no seats! There is no idolatry on the part of their followers, simply a delight to experience the moving out in the power of the supernatural. It has not escaped my notice also that the greater the humility the more effective the ministry.

Frankly I never saw the Holy Spirit offend anyone. When I hear Christians in Churches where the sovereignty of the Holy Spirit is not in evidence, say "We've got to take it gently, folks get offended!" I'm inclined to reply that the Holy Spirit, both gentle and powerful, never offended any genuine Christian. He is so sensitive, and if people get offended then they have a real problem. It is that they need deliverance!

So we have in Mark 1 evidence that demons recognised Jesus. Also we see in the scriptures that sickness was frequently dealt with at the same time as casting out demons.

E.g. in dumbness, deafness, blindness and infirmity. We have seen many times patients healed when the demon was cast out, and they needed no further treatment.

What Else Do Demons Do?

1. Demons entice, (tempt usually verbally or with the eyes)
    Example:

a) A man in his office constantly notices the pretty office girl sitting on the corner of a desk in close proximity to his. She sits swinging her feet clad in high heels and nylon stockings, her dress has a low cleavage. Every time the man looks up she is looking in his direction. He is married, so is she. A voice says in his ears 'Ask her out to lunch. She is interested in you!'

b) A lady, walking down a street finds a wallet on the pavement. She happens to be very short of money. The contents are a wad of notes. She looks around. There is not a soul in sight. A voice says, 'Keep it, nobody has seen you.'

2. Demons harass. (They know your movements, where you are going or have been)
    Example:

a) A businessman leaves his place of employment after a hard day at his office, only to find that his car has a puncture. He furiously changes the wheel which causes him to arrive late on the now congested motorway. He is very tired and very late home. Upon arrival he finds that his meal is spoiled and the children are misbehaving. Finally he explodes! The demon of anger which has hovered around him all day and has followed him home, finally enters the man and manifests.

3. Demons Torment. (Usually attacking through torturous thoughts and in the realm of the mind)
    Example:

a) A man has opened the post to find that a friend he owes a fair sum of money cannot hang around for repayment any longer. The man is already faced with payment demands on overdue gas bill, telephone bill and school fees. He has no means of meeting his debts and fear gets in (fear hath torment 1 John 4:18). He sees the heating and telephone cut off, as the day progresses he imagines that his children will be forced to attend a state school and that as a result his wife will leave him because private education was such a priority for her. He will not be able to tell her that money is not forthcoming because he has his friend on the trail for the loan to be repaid instantly. The end of the day finds him unable to swallow his evening meal and his dreams in bed that night are of the bankruptcy court. He awakes exhausted after disturbed sleep. Satan renews attack immediately.

b) A young woman had ended a torrid and passionate affair because she has given her life to Jesus. Her body is missing the satisfaction she felt she knew in her affair. She is in bed alone with her thoughts. Night after night she is faced with the problem not evident when she is busy during the daytime. She is resisting masturbation with all her strength, but finally feels that this release would be better than contacting her old boyfriend. She thinks it will be just this once until her desire subsides, but it never does. The demon of lust is manifesting. She continues in the habit.

4. Demons Compel. (Smoking, drinking, handwashing, garrulity – [excessive talking], anorexia, bulimia, masturbation.)

Note. Some of these are more socially acceptable than others, but there is no real difference in needing to reach out for the T.V. switch when you enter a room than there is in reaching out for a cigarette or gin! Television is the plug-in drug! Many are addicted to it, sitting mesmerised by rubbish night after night. Television is also a time-wasting spirit!

Inability to resist satisfying any habit.

Example:

a) A lady with a sweet tooth resists buying sweets in the supermarket, having wheeled the trolley all round avoiding the biscuits, cake and confectionery shelves – but she cannot resist picking up one of the chocolate bars displayed by the checkout. She was almost out of the shop! Her eyes saw the chocolate!

b) Two old friends meet in the street and greet each other with an identical 'How are you?' They both go to answer at the same time, laugh, and one lady steps back to allow the other politely to proceed. However she never gets a word in because the friend rattles on both asking her questions and answering for her. The tongue spirit of garrulity is in evidence. People who will not allow you to get a word in, talk over you, interrupt, ignore what you have said and continue with their own debates and viewpoint. You see them eager to have you finish a sentence and get in with their own comments. Two way discussion or conversation is impossible. Beware witchcraft!

5. Demons enslave (driving forces that cannot be resisted). Sexual sin is a common area, lust, compulsive masturbation, speeding in cars. Overeating and vomiting as in anorexia bulimia, alcoholism. 4 & 5 can be bracketed together as demons of addiction.

Example:

a) Drivers who cannot pull away slowly at the traffic lights but must go WHOOM! Speeding – unable to drive a car unless at top speed.

b) One lady reported to me that she knew a road in a town which has five restaurants. She would gorge a meal in the first. Order a meal in the next. Whilst waiting for it to be served she would visit the lavatory – contract her stomach muscles, spew the meal up from the previous restaurant, go and eat, then move to the next restaurant repeating the procedure until she had worked her way up the street. Unbelievable but true. This was an actual case of a spirit of anorexia bulimia of nineteen years duration. Cast out four years ago the person is still free. Victims can take laxatives, emetics, put their fingers or other objects down their throats or simply contract their abdominal muscles with great skill to make them vomit.

6. Demons defile (make feel dirty, inject dirty thoughts especially at prayer time).

Example:

a) One adult, a victim of incest at twelve years of age, would swim every day. She disliked swimming but it was the only thing she could do which made her feel clean.

b) A lady who had real problems with a deep rooted unclean spirit said that every time she attempted to take the cup at communion as she opened her mouth to sip the wine the devil would present her with a perverted picture of Jesus. This almost made her feel insane. She was very distressed. This was a very difficult case as much lust, fantasy and unclean spirits had been dealt with, but deliverance was not complete until several ruler demons of lust (Prince Asmodeus, Demas, Articus were cast out in Jesus' name). One needs to seek a word of knowledge in such cases and that was what I did in this case.

Note: When patients report such horrific details, however sickened you may be in the natural, be certain to rest in the love of the Lord Jesus and remember Satan is so vile he can think up the most iniquitous insults and torment – both to shock you and to destroy. People who confess such terrible matters should be highly esteemed in Christ Jesus for doing so. It is not an easy matter, as one would easily understand.

7. Demons deceive. (A spirit of pride opens the way for a spirit of deception, self deception, and lying spirits).

Note: Persons with a physical stiff neck or torticollis (Wry neck) should do a study from their concordance on stiff neck – for illustrations on the evidence of a resident spirit of pride.

Example:

a) People who are never wrong, always know better and have the last word, are invariably self-deceived.

b) People taken in by false prophecy, flattery, falsehood in any area, matrimonial deception (adultery), deception in medicine (homoeopathy, iridology, acupuncture, dowsing etc) deception in Churches (much of the faith and prosperity message which persuades people they can pray in a mink coat, a fortune, or a Rolls Royce) counterfeit healing (spiritualism).

Note: There are master spirits of deception. These are they which are so convincing to many. Freemasons which appear to be involved in good works, homoeopathy which appears to heal, are two such master spirits. A master spirit has a very definite seducing spirit attached to it. Men who are nothing to look at but seem to conquer every woman in sight usually have master spirits of deception. One usually finds that they are also conmen, conning their employers and every one they come into contact with. They have a very convincing air and are like the Orion spirit (Job 38:31), charming with charisma. They often know the scriptures and can convey the gospel extremely well.

8. Demons weaken (make sick and infirm – then it is easier to occupy).

Example:

a) Christians who allow themselves to be drained and strained by their ministries, become tired and then exhausted. Sickness follows and the spirit of infirmity gets in. Satan seeks to wear out the Saints!

Notes on driving: It is no good praying the blood of Jesus over your car and getting into it and speeding. If you break the laws of the land you may not claim your soteria (deliverance from temporal evil Hebrews 1:14). I do not know the speed limits of foreign countries, but the angels fall off at 71mph in Britain! Remember that! Protection is ours only if we are obedient. We may not agree with the speed limit but as Christians we must observe it. We may not approve of the government, but as Christians we must pray for those who govern us (1 Timothy 2:1-3).

What are Demons?

They are disembodied persons with a passionate desire to get into people, or animals as a second choice.

Two Objects of Demons

1. To keep you from knowing Jesus Christ as your Saviour.
2. If you do know Jesus, to keep you from serving Him effectively.

Satan, as I have said already, seeks to wear out the Saints to make then infirm and unable to serve Jesus as effectively as they would or should.

Dying to Self and the Flesh

Man is in many respects governed by lusts of the flesh. That is why fasting is so important. Lust also covers many fleshly appetites. What about the mushrooming of health and fitness centres in Britain? I had to use a gym in one such following my accident. The spirit of idolatry reigned supreme over that place. Body worship! We have to die to the flesh absolutely and come out of the world. If we keep astride the fence with one foot in the world it becomes a very uncomfortable place to be. The flesh is our lower nature.

Derek Prince gives the example of the illustration of the vulture and the carcass. Flesh is the carcass, a demon is the vulture feeding off it. The lower we fall in our fleshly nature through disobedience, the closer becomes the invasion of demons. I expect you have seen one of those beautiful natural history films on Africa, where for example the buffalo or wildebeest weakling in the herd gets sick and cut off from the herd. It stumbles to its knees. Vultures appear from nowhere and perch on nearby rocks or trees awaiting the animal's demise. From its knees the animal keels over onto its side or back, the vultures fly from the higher branches of the trees to the lower, to be in closer proximity as the creature endures its final death throes. The moment life is ebbing away they descend to hack the flesh off the carcass.

So it is when people sink to what we call the lowest

of the low in their nature. For example, a couple are already having sexual relations outside marriage. Then that gets boring, so they invite the stimulation of pornography into their sex life. After a while this palls and they resort to alcohol or drugs to get a higher stimulation. They are sinking lower and lower and demons are entering in their hordes. Like the Mafia they go in gangs and there are numerous demons of lust (See Deliverance, The Children's Bread by Robert Ellender).

Summing up of Demonic Characteristics

It is one word: **Restlessness**. Demonised people have no peace, they cannot relax or settle. They always have to be involved in some pastime or fruitless pursuit. It may be legitimate. That does not matter. Such people always have to be going somewhere, doing something, driving here and there maybe with no purpose, shopping for things they do not need or want simply because they cannot relax and do nothing.

They may even feel guilty sitting in a chair doing nothing! Many people spend endless hours creating beautiful homes and gardens and never enjoying them because they cannot sit still in them. They cannot be alone and seek constant company or diversion.

The need to be silent or inactive is unknown to them. They have no peace. Proverbs 25:28 says *"He that hath no rule over his own spirit is like a city that is broken down and without walls."*

Hyperactivity and restlessness leaves no space for prayer and meditation on Jesus. Spiritual defences are built up in prayer, silence and thanksgiving in that silence. Physical inactivity can mean real spiritual activity and spiritual refreshment, contact with God. If spiritual walls are not built, anything may invade. Check on the mortar daily.

Make space, treasure it what ever you do, do not allow anything to squeeze out that precious time with our Lord. I have learned to say "no", not to be available, and to take the telephone off the hook.

I am aware that the anointing depends entirely upon continual closeness to the Lord and contact with the Holy Spirit. It is a constant battle, a spiritual warfare to preserve space for the Father, Son and Holy Spirit. I praise the Lord for the time I recognised that to be true. Servanthood includes being fit to serve!

The demands on my time increase every month, every week, every day. I know they are not going to get less and to cope I need more of my Maker. Anyone in ministry will tell you the same thing.

It is also vanity to believe that only you have the answer to people's laments. That's why I so enjoy teaching others to "Go And Do Likewise", because I foresee the day when I shall stop and get on my face full time for Israel. I have been obedient to the call to deliverance ministry. I am also aware that God can stop me any time He desires to do so. So I am listening and watching as never before. Be encouraged, it is easier as you practice it!

Chapter 21

Areas of Residence

Demons reside in:

1. **The Emotions** (attitudes) eg, anger, self pity, pride, jealousy, attention seeking, etc.
2. **Root Problems** (rejection) can lead to the curse of the root of bitterness – misery, despair, ugliness, loneliness, self rejection, etc.

Note: When these 'misery' spirits are passive they can lead to a spirit of death, a death wish, a pining away because they are not being resisted. When these spirits are active they may lead to a suicidal spirit or death. One has to discern if a suicidal spirit is an attention seeking spirit. Have you ever said, 'I don't want to live,' or 'I wish I was dead.' Then stop now and turn to Psalm 118:17. "*I shall not die, but live and declare the works of the Lord.*"

Put this book down, take your Bible, stand up and make this proclamation, boldly several times. Say it positively and with authority. Release yourself from the curse which you spoke over yourself when you spoke out your death wish.

When you say "I do not want to live", you are giving a personal invitation to Satan to kill you. As a child of eleven and twice more in my life before I was thirty, I tried very definitely to commit suicide. The third time I was actually pronounced dead in the hospital theatre. I was pregnant and I know that this had a diabolical effect on my son who was ultimately born.

I carried the guilt of it all for many years. I did not want to give birth to a child when I knew that my former husband did not love me.

A team of women whom I had taught the ministry ultimately ministered to me in great power. I submitted to their ministry to me and it was an incredible evening for which I was so grateful to God. It was indeed a precious and humbling time for me because I was deeply moved as Angela my personal intercessor led these lovely women, all taught at the Clinic, moving out in power under the anointing, that Jesus might set me free. There were visions, words of knowledge and revelation of sores I had kept long hidden. I share these things openly to encourage you all.

I had fasted three days beforehand and so had they. During that fast I had packed up an enormous and very expensive collection of lead crystal which had been given to me by a person whom I subsequently realized was very demonised and whose ancestors were also under a terrible curse of insanity and death. I had hung onto this last one of my priceless possessions even after I had received the revelation that it was cursed. The problem was that I had bought two crystal cabinets to house it at the time I received this gift and I did not want them empty. I was not then trusting that my Father could give me something of greater value, something more priceless – freedom from torment!

The girls had absolutely no idea about any of this. Nor did I reveal that I had emptied the crystal cabinets before they arrived!

During that ministry which went on for many hours about thirty deeply hidden demons and many spoken curses over my life were dealt with in Jesus' name. I was finally on the floor and a spirit of death had been called out. Every addictive drug spirit was called out, spirits of Librium, Valium, Nembutal, Distalgesic, Morphine, Pethadine, Paracetamol, Ergotamine etc. Every homoeopathic remedy, spirits of arnica, phosphorous, lachessis, pulsatilla, kali phos, natrum mur, sepia and so on.

By this time I was on the floor and everything was very hazy. I knew I was not free. I was aware of their incredible love and their bending over me. Angela said, "you are not quite free, is there a block?"

I recall moaning that they should pray for a word of knowledge and hearing them all praying in the Spirit. Their voices got farther and farther away.

Then I became aware as Susanna leaned over me and asked, "Does the word crystal mean anything?"

They told me that I let out a terrible scream and the curse of the crystal was broken over me.

Susanna related later that she got the word crystal and was waiting for the word ball to follow it. She was the new member of our team. Then the Holy Spirit said to her that it was not a crystal ball and certainly I had never used one or had one used on me.

I then explained about the crystal and later took them downstairs to show it to them. You may imagine how delighted we all were. What is more the Lord refilled my crystal cabinet in a miraculous way. In Penang in 1987 Dr. Joy Seevaratnam said he kept seeing something like a shining glittering star in my home which concerned him. Did I have any such stars? I said no. But on the base of each piece of lead crystal I saw that there was a glittering star!!

To me it is a reminder of God's mercy that He used me so mightily in ministry in spite of my being such a mess and needing so much deliverance myself. I do give Him all the glory and praise for the miracles he has wrought in me. When I know what I was and what I am now – it is quite difficult to recognise myself, and many others now are passing the same comments.

So if you are struggling out there – have faith. God may set you free in layers as He did me, and has many others.

If you are wondering why I am interspersing this teaching with such comments, it's because it is exactly what I do when I teach. People are interested in genuine life experiences to encourage them. So many wrote to me about my first book. "I couldn't put it down it was so real".

Other Areas of Residence

3. **Rebellion**
   (is as witchcraft 1 Samuel 15:23) eg resentment, hatred, anger, violence, aggression. These are all typical gang leader characteristics.)

4. **The Mind**
   (battle field) eg doubt, unbelief, confusion, indecision, double mindedness, depression, insanity.

Note: Satan will tell you, you have no money in the bank, you are a failure, no one likes you.

   Put on the helmet of salvation which covers the mind and cast down all imaginations and have the mind of Christ. (2 Corinthians 10:4-5, 1 Corinthians 2:16).

5. **The Tongue**
   Lying, cheating, exaggeration, blasphemy (in speech and swearing), garrulity, criticism and gossip (often two Church going demons).

6. **Sexual Area**
   Remember that sex is good, it was designed by God who saw that it was good between man and wife. All compulsive sexual aberrations are demonic. Homosexuality, lesbianism, fornication, adultery, effeminacy, oral sex, group sex etc.

7. **Lusts**
   Perverted desires or appetites. 1 John 2:16 speaks of the lust of the flesh and the lust of the eyes. Men who cannot take their eyes off womens' breasts, legs or whatever. There is demonic power in control with the eyes, e.g. mesmerism, hypnosis, even staring continuously, can be dangerous. I have been astonished at the hidden lust in Christian men and women. It is a real problem. Confess it, repent of it and get rid of it. Don't indulge in guilt or self condemnation.

Note: Gluttony can be lust – a serious problem in the Church – foodaholics. Remember all addictions grow on frustration. Have a drink, have a coffee, have a cookie, have a chocolate, have a smoke, have a drug. There is little difference but some are more socially acceptable.

I was addicted to Mars bars and cream doughnuts. The doughnuts addiction came a few years ago when a new country supermarket branch opened locally. My first visit was greeted by the smell of doughnuts being baked on the premises, I was lured to the counter. I do not eat cakes and biscuits or what I call goo! Satan must have caught me off guard. I bought not one but two topped with jam and cream – in a cellophane wrapper. I told myself it would be nice to have one in the freezer in case anyone called because I didn't keep biscuits. But I ate both in the car, they did not get home! This happened repeatedly when I visited that store. I did not even enjoy the doughnuts, I knew that the aroma was causing me to fancy those cream filled concoctions.

Finally I took control of the situation in Jesus' name. As I hurried to that counter one day I stopped. I gripped one of the shelves with tinned vegetables and bound the lust for doughnuts and hung on there praying into the situation in the Spirit, loosing self-control into my inner man! I also asked the Lord to make me revolted by the smell. That was the end of it. I have never wanted one since. It seems quite ridiculous. It seems such a little thing – but that's how Satan gets in – in little ways!

8. **Seducing spirits**

Jezebel spirit, (dresses to attract men, short skirts, low neckline, heavy make up. Masses of jewellery and eye shadow. The Jezebel spirit is a spirit of manipulation, domination and control).

Note: Watch for witchcraft and mediumship in females who outline and extend their eyelids with black or dark pencil. Let the Lord change your make-up ladies!

9. **Ahab spirit**

Opposite of Jezebel spirit. The man who is laid back cannot make decisions in the home, leaves it to the wife. She will often say he is simple and handle everything. He hands the financial reins to his wife, overtly for the sake of peace and quiet. Watch also for the male spirit in his wife!

10. The occult

A vast realm which would take twenty pages – includes Yoga, ouija board, Dungeons and Dragons games, tarot cards, clairvoyance, mind reading, tea leaves, crystal balls, martial arts, transcendental meditation, levitation, dowsing, iridology, palmistry, fantasy games, rôle-playing war games, etc, etc. See Robert Ellender's hand book on "Deliverance: the Children's Bread," for a complete list.

11. False Religions.

Islam, Budhism, Hinduism, Dragon or Bird of Paradise worship (male and female Chinese gods), Jehovah witnesses, Spiritualism, Christian Science, Mormonism etc.

12. Heresies.

Armstrongism, Church of God, (provides "Plain Truth" magazine), Food fetishes (non fads), Refraining from certain foods on scriptural grounds.

13. Physical Bodies.

Epilepsy, Arthritis (can often be unforgiveness), stiff neck (often pride), tics, deformity, crippling, club foot, multiple tics, (Gilles de la Tourette Syndrome), fits etc.

Note: Gilles de la Tourette Syndrome – severe generalized multiple tics beginning in boyhood coprolalia – obscene speech and spitting. Club foot was found by one minister to be an ancestral spirit of bestiality.

Caution

Never focus on the manifestation of a demon – but on the reality of Jesus Christ.

Chapter 22

How To Be Delivered

1. Be humble (if dignity is more important – forget it!).
2. Be honest (call it what it is – abortion is a spirit of murder).
3. Confess faith in Christ – make Him the High Priest of your confession.
4. Confess any known (or unknown sin) by self or ancestors (we do not always know what our ancestors were involved in, so just name the known sins and add "all unknown sins").
5. Repent of all sin; without Godly repentance – deliverance is not on. (Prov 28:13). *He that covereth his sins shall not prosper: but whoso confesseth and forsaketh them shall have mercy.*
6. Break with the occult and all secret societies (eg freemasonry, buffaloes, odd fellows, druids).
7. Forgive others, everyone absolutely (in enlightened self interest).

Note: As I have already mentioned some people will have great difficulty in doing this, especially those victims of incest who feel so betrayed by parents meant to protect them. Remind these unhappy people that harbouring hatred causes one to be cursed, that we need to bless those who despitefully use us. (Matthew 5:44, Luke 6:28). We also tell people that the Bible tells us overcome evil with good and that if we do the Lord actually rewards us (Romans 12:19-22, Proverbs 25:21-22). Then lead them in the prayer I have already set out in chapter 17.

Expelling Demons

In Greek and Hebrew the same word pneuma means spirit and breath, so it seems quite in order to breathe the evil or unclean spirits out. Please do it slowly and deeply. Little puffs which would not blow the skin off a rice pudding will not avail! Mean business. You are getting rid of something vile. Expelling demons is not a passive affair. Also when you are calling out demons in the name of Jesus, make certain the person being ministered to is not praying in the Holy Spirit. If the Word of God is on someone's lips a demon exiting via the mouth will not bypass it.

It may take several breaths before the demon leaves. This is where the gift of the discerning of spirits is vital. The person ministering will discern when the evil spirit no longer occupies and move on to commanding the next spirit to leave in Jesus' name.

Watch out for the demons of slumber and sleep coming into full play just before ministry or when you are teaching. If I see people nodding off and discern the demon of slumber and sleep I bind it before I go on teaching. Likewise spirits of doubt and unbelief may have to be bound.

Jesus never explained to us where demons come from but we do know that they walk about the dry places and are looking for appropriate physical forms to manifest in.

Get the person receiving ministry to deeply inhale the Holy Spirit with an inward breath through the nostrils when deliverance is finished. If the spirit of grief and mourning has been cast out, bind up the broken heart. When the ministry is complete anoint the person with oil. I use olive oil and anoint them in the name of Jesus Christ.

When the person is rested ask them to get to their feet, raise their hands to God and praise Him for their deliverance. I usually get the person to say three times each

"I praise you Lord that I am free. I praise you Lord that I am healed – and I give Jesus all the glory. Thank you Jesus".

Jesus loves to be thanked.

I also recommend that people continue to acknowledge their deliverance and healing for a month when they rise in the morning. By the time they have spoken out these words of praise and thanksgiving for one month, they will know that they are free.

Note: Deliverance may take more than one session.

Chapter 23

Hindrances and Failure to Walk in Deliverance

1. Lack of repentance.
2. Lack of desperation (passivity).
3. Wrong motives (James 4:3 – *Ye ask, and receive not, because ye ask amiss, that ye may consume it upon your lusts*).
4. Self-centredness – desire for attention.
   (Chronic cases who never want to be delivered because it is the only time they are the centre of the stage).
5. Failure to break with the occult, or rid oneself or home of occult objects.

E.g. Ornaments, buddhas, crucifixes (Christ is not on the cross, He is risen!) rosaries, lucky horseshoes, heather, rabbits feet, charms, wishbones, cornish pixies etc. Bangles made from elephant hair, ivory (can you say that the elephant is not cursed? Look at their horrific history). Jade. For jewellery and ornaments, Jade is blessed on the floors of Chinese temples before being carved into jewellery and ornaments. Have you seen the bone china models, ancient and very modern, of gypsies reading the palms of lovely maidens, or delicate bone china maidens reading crystal balls? Colour supplements of national newspapers are doing a roaring trade in these at present. There are very old china ornaments by famous potteries selling these antiques and their modern counterparts. BEWARE! IT IS WRITTEN if you bring an accursed thing into your house, you become an accursed thing. (Deuteronomy 7:26).

Statues of Mary and the child, busts of famous men.

Psalm 135:18. *They that make them are like unto them: so is every one that trusteth in them.*

Are you trusting in lucky charms or talismen? Do you kneel and pray to Mary, kiss the toes or relics of Saints? It is written in the commandments – Deuteronomy 5:7-9: *thou shalt have no other gods before me.*

7. *Thou shalt have no other gods before Me.*

8. *Thou shalt not make thee any graven image, or any likeness of any thing that is in heaven above, or that is in the earth beneath, or that is in the waters beneath the earth.*

9. *Thou shalt not bow down thyself unto them, nor serve them: for I the Lord thy God am a jealous God, visiting the iniquity of the fathers upon the children unto the third and fourth generation of them that hate me.*

How about that? I think God makes it quite clear.

Even consider your gold cross and chain. I have lost count of the crosses and chains which have been removed following the teach-in with resultant blessing – an outstanding one of which I shall relate later in this book.

I had a lovely heavy gold cross and chain. They were bought separately. The man when he fastened it around my neck spoke a curse over me as he did.

"I've bought you this to chain you to me." I was immediately in bondage to him.

It took me ten years to get free. I thought it was a lovely thing at the time. I had always wanted a nice heavy gold chain. The fact that it was a high ranking freemason who put it around my neck didn't help. Dear me. Hosea 4:6!! *My people are destroyed for lack of knowledge:* Later a lovely chunky plain gold cross was added to it. Quite an expensive piece of jewellery it was, and antique.

When John Edwards, bless him, was praying

deliverance for me concerning the spirit of homoeopathy, he saw it around my neck. I saw him looking, plucked it away from my throat proudly saying as I held it towards him.

"Look, it is not a crucifix."

He replied "No, I see, but would you agree that the Cross is the place of execution?"

Naturally I answered yes and he continued:

"Do you really want to walk about with a gallows around your neck?" Well, that was another piece to be melted down for the Church! I was never so glad to be shot of anything! Praise the Lord for that man's visit.

He went on to say that if one really wanted to identify with Jesus and the cross the only one to wear would be a very large heavy wooden one."

This witness has set so many people free who were fearful to go out without their cross or crucifix. If being without it bothers you – alas, it has become a lucky charm. So get rid of that St. Christopher off your car, bracelet or whatever.

Carvings of dragons or elephants and African or other carvings must be regarded with great suspicion. Elephants are worshipped for their memory and strength. Any unforgiveness or brute strength in your family? Anyone who says, "I'll forgive but never forget"? The dragon and the bird of paradise are Chinese gods, worshipped in pagan rituals. The devil is also called the dragon. Snakes. Have you got draught excluders or doorsteps which are stuffed cotton snakes? Vases where the handles are serpents? Is not that another name for Satan?? Snake jewellery is all the rage, snake rings with ruby eyes, statues of martial arts or wrestlers? When I saw my son's girlfriend return from Greece with a couple of cobras dangling in her ears I shuddered. What tempted Eve?

I had a woman patient come to the Clinic one day. She was Indonesian. She sat before me and my eyes riveted on a fat heavy gold cobra around her neck.

"Take that off please", I requested.

112

"Don't you like it?"

"No, with one of those around your neck no wonder you have a throat problem".

She unfastended it and trickled it onto my desk in a coil.

"In Jesus' name," I said, "get that off my desk and out of the Clinic." She then popped it in her bag but I made her take it out to her car. She returned, by which time I was discerning Subud, which is a cult.

She did not return after the next visit. The presence of the Holy Spirit in the Clinic is sometimes too much for those people. Frankly, I feel relieved to see them go. We continue:

6. Failure to confess specific sins such as abortion (check for the spirit of murder).

7. Failure to sever evil soulish relationships (Derek Prince says 'binding and gooey!').

8. Being under a curse.

9. Not separated by water baptism. Israel was separated by the water of the Red Sea. If you are not baptized by immersion you do not qualify to stay free.

10. Being part of a larger battle requiring corporate action. People made ill by wrong or strife in Churches etc.

Note:

Pierced ears. Answer these questions.

1. Did God make you with holes in your ears?

2. Could making holes in your ears be called mutilation? (or in your nose for that matter).
   Quite a lot of money is made by doctors who pierce labia of females to make them feel erotic. This is fact.

3. Did you know that slaves were pinned to the doorposts by rings in their ears?

4. Are you in bondage to anyone or anything? Smoking, alcohol, sexual sin?

5. Are you in bondage to food or any habit, even washing on Monday, ironing on Tuesday, shopping on Wednesday?

If bondage is not your problem then it may not matter if you can get over thinking you have improved on God's handiwork by adding a couple of holes!

I have seen the aforementioned problems dealt with, by the removal of jewellery or rings from pierced ears. I praise God that mine would not pierce. My earlobes always went septic. My former fiancé, who insisted that I should be fashionable and have pierced ears, said mine went septic because they were improperly pierced. He was adamant that he would do it in his operating theatre. So I succumbed and my lobes swelled up and were ten times as septic.

Isn't God merciful? I guess at that time in my life He thought I had enough bondage. Loving Father!

Chapter 24

How to Keep Deliverance, How Demons Enter and Lesser Known Spirits

How to keep deliverance

1. Make Jesus Lord.
2. Put on the garment of praise (Isaiah 61).
3. Put on the full armour of God (Ephesians 6).
4. Live by God's Word. FACTS, FAITH, FEELINGS. The facts are the Word of God, the faith is what you get from hearing, knowing, studying and understanding the Word, and your feelings come in order only as a result. That is the order. FACTS, FAITH, FEELINGS. So many put feelings first. Do that and you are sunk!
5. Submit to God – resist the devil and he will flee (James 4:7).
6. Keep the right fellowship. Beware the company you keep (1 John 1:7).
7. Come under discipline, self discipline, school discipline, work discipline, church discipline. You are not free to indulge in whims and fancies. Any problems, get in the closet.
8. Make Jesus central. (John 12:31-32). 31: *Now is the judgement of the world: now shall the prince of this world be cast out.* 32: *And I if I be lifted up from the earth I will draw all men unto me.*

Focus on Jesus, Not on Demons!
How Demons Enter

1. Occult board games, ancestral involvement with the occult. A vast area which includes spiritualism, horoscopes, freemasonry, etc.

2. Pre-natal influence in the womb. e.g. shock in pregnancy – fear enters the woman or baby and usually comes out at birth with the child. Rejection, a child in utero knows if it is not wanted or is an inconvenient conception. (See the hidden hyperactive spirit in Chapter 15 of "Go and Do Likewise.")

4. Soulish domination. People who dominate, control and manipulate others. Mothers dominating children, especially sons. The spiritual umbilical cord needs cutting in Jesus' name. If the child is a little devil the mother is likely to be a witch!

5. Pressure in early childhood. James 3:16. *For where envying and strife is, there is confusion and every evil work.* Parents rowing or indulging in verbal or physical abuse can be responsible for invasion of children by evil spirits.

6. Through grief. Loss of a child, parent, loved one, betrayal, ending of engagement, disappointment. Even loss of a fortune or a beloved home can cause the spirit of grief and mourning to enter.

7. Physical weakness opens the door to spirits of infirmity and others will follow. So look after that temple of the Holy Spirit. Build up the walls with prayer and fasting, keep the mortar new. Ask yourself too:

   Would I put into my car what I put into my body and expect a good performance? We often take greater care of our cars or washing machines, making certain they get the right oil, petrol or powder! Fresh air and exercise are also important. Don't get stale in the central heating. Don't exhaust yourself locking yourself up with that home computer. I can assure you that the computer has a spirit which is a ruler and controlling demon. They are addictive and daylight robbers!

8. Sinful habits. Persist in the habit and it becomes demonic. Pornographic or blue films, masturbation, fornication, etc.

Lesser Known Spirits

The Orion spirit

The Orion spirit is Lucifer's lieutenant, his right-hand man. It is the Prince Charming spirit and has great charisma and conviction. It is the spirit of a religious act, not to be confused with a religious spirit which is unattractive. The Orion spirit is attractive to many. The Orion spirit is a great narrator, a seducing spirit silky in every respect, which dresses differently to attract and covers all its belongings with "Jesus is Lord", "Don't follow me, follow Jesus", stickers etc. No stone is left unturned to advertise its religiosity and it is a superb and gifted orator, witty, entertaining and seductive. It is deceptive, self-deceptive, hypnotic and has great vanity. It is strongly supported and aided by the Leviathan, or crocodile spirit (Job 41 AV) which is the monarch of all pride. Part of the deception of this spirit is that it may pretend to be very humble indeed; sometimes lust is attendant on it.

Spirit of slime

Invariably coming in as a transference of spirits from the root spirit lust and fornication. It sticks to one, causes heaviness and inexplicable depression. Associated with frog, toad and serpentine spirits. Has been observed in the spirit seeping in and over everything or fastened to a person in pendulous fashion, where the bag of slime is droplet shaped and although thin at the neck will not snap off but weighs the person down heavier and heavier. It contaminates and those oppressed by it often blame themselves for the way they feel, so it brings in self condemnation. Can be resultant of any sexual excess, masturbation, etc. Transfers very easily. May exit as slime from any orifice.

Rat spirit

This is a gnawing spirit, like the spirit of cancer it can eat one away. Usually nibbles and goes away and returns for more. A very destructive spirit causing all manner of physical disease. It is a nit picking, critical spirit, a tale bearer, attaches blame to anyone but itself. Often accuses you of hiding its property. "Where did you put my?" to person who could not possibly have touched it. It is a hoarding spirit, filling its hole (den, home, place of work) with clutter it can never use or does not need. Doubles up on possessions one normally has one of. Can be a compulsive purchaser. Loves secret hiding places, will bolt when under attack.

Elephant god spirit

This spirit is thick skinned about everyone else's feelings but super sensitive about its own hurts. There is much pride and it remembers every detail of every hurt it ever suffered. It has brute force when aroused and its strength is not dependent on its size. Like the Python spirit it is crushing and absolutely ruthless. It charges over anything and anybody trampling underfoot by devious means anything that gets in the way of it achieving its own desires. Rarely gets physically ill but can be mentally deranged.

Chapter 25

The Manifestation of Evil Spirits

There will not be space to deal with the manifestation of all spirits. Also do not *look* for the manifestation as they may not be obvious, except to those ministering with a sharp gift of the discernment of spirits, who can see the demon leave, through the eyes or any orifice. You may see parts of the body swell, lumps in the throat, angry staring eyes, change in skin colour. I once saw a lady purple with pride. One of my staff was bending over her wearing a purple silk blouse. It was difficult to see the difference between her skin and the blouse!

The spirit of death

Usually they fall into a death like pose, neatly folding their hands over their chest, very straight body as though in a coffin. The skin is usually ashen. Years ago when I first experienced a patient manifesting like this I had to take her pulse!! Please do not rearrange the hands and body – make certain the spirit is leaving – a guide is that the colour returns, breathing becomes more obvious.

The spirit of masturbation

In both males and females will exit through the hands with tingling and numbness. The medical profession will tell you that constant masturbation causes the hands to go numb. Hands are usually locked and stiff and icy cold. The person may start shaking the hands and telling the spirit to go as they beat them in the air frantically.

The spirit of violence

Flaring eyes, will tower over you angrily. (Don't fear, keep standing, I've had six foot six inches towering over my five foot two inches!) They may attack you but this in my experience is rare, however, I have seen pieces of heavy furniture tossed in the air with brute strength, from a very small man. Violence may roar or stare fiercely.

The spirit of anger and rage

Will roar, sweat, glare, growl, grind teeth, threaten, go red and bloated in the face, veins standing out on the nose. (Keep standing – greater is He that is within you.) Similar to violence and, if serious, restrain.

The mocking spirit

Will laugh in your face, ridicule you, scoff. Do not worry about this, it has to go in Jesus' name.

Grief and mourning

Wails, sobs, cries very heartbrokenly. After infilling remember to bind up the broken heart.

Infirmity

Terrible weakness may overtake the person, they may sink down and tell you they are tired.

Sulleness

Will do nothing, will not co-operate.

Fear

Will exhibit terror, often shows in eyes and throat, may scream, tremble, weep, etc.

Deprivation

May throw clothes off. Stop this.

Pride

Exhibits stiff neck, face colours or swells, haughty. May

fold arms defiantly.

Serpentine, snake, python spirits
See Chapter 35 of "Go and do Likewise". Can twine and twist or slither about exactly like a snake. I have seen people rear up just like serpents with tongues darting, or spitting or hissing. On one occasion those present thought they were in the snake pit.

Homosexual spirit
May prance about in an effeminate manner. On two occasions I was led to call out a mincing spirit in former homosexuals, and the result was quite amazing. A prancing with short steps and fanned out hands, a total change in manner and voice occurred.

Roman Catholic spirits
Mariology, mariolatry (Mary worship). Each time these came out of the ears with great pain. Quite often people look as though they are wired up to the electric chair.

The spirit of Death and Hades
Comes out with great violence, blood and mucus from the mouth on one occasion, always seems to be a violent exit.

Spirit of lust and fornication
May dribble, pant, produce slime.

Transference of spirits
Normally occurs when two people have sexual or close contact. Can also "rub off" on those sharing houses, or living in close proximity or friendship where one really loves, cares, or esteems the other. Contamination can come when, for example, the spirit of lust in one recognizes the deep hidden covered up lust in the person it is in close contact with, causing arousal of a lust not normally obvious in the sufferer. Often the most prim matronly or innocent types harbour unrecognized lust, and so fall easy prey to

active lust by tranference of spirits. This is the seducing spirit which causes others to behave out of character or against their natural and spiritual inclination. Transference can be from parent to innocent offspring. Fear transfers causing panic in crowds etc. These are all general observations in seven years of ministry. I do *not* pretend that they are typical. One can only report on what one has seen in one's own ministry and in observing the ministry of others. Discharge of slime, reported by Derek Prince as being the nest of the demon, may be coughed or vomited up. Particularly I have noticed this in sexual spirits. Please do not address demons unless you are led by the Holy Spirit to do so. I have only done this rarely and each time the spirit identified itself or said it was not coming out.

Religious spirits are extremely difficult at times. Also there are the spirits of reluctance and hesitation, doubt and unbelief, time wasting spirits and attention seeking spirits to be on guard for. Clown or jester spirits are artificially brave quite often.

I have carefully listened to the teaching of men and women I consider to be experts in this field and learned that we should not question what the Holy Spirit gives us. In 1988 I ministered to a lady and the Holy Spirit gave me a mute spirit. I called it out. The lady's mouth opened so wide and she appeared to want to scream quite desperately but could not do so until the spirit came out with a terrible scream, after a long struggling silence. In 1989 another layer was being peeled off this particular lady when I found myself coming against a mute spirit again. I thought to myself that surely this had been dealt with a year previously. But it was the same pattern. She sank to her feet, rolled over on her side, her mouth was locked open as though in voiceless agony. Finally, and it was a long time, it departed with a blood curdling scream. This was after a teach-in and not a few people jumped! About three months later, I ministered to this lady again. Incest had surfaced by this time and I was so amazed to find myself coming up against a mute spirit again.

She was by then one of my team. I knew I was not deceived. Satan starts to prod you with a suggestion that you did not get it out the first time! The lady's mouth was so unbelievably wide open we could almost see down into her gut! Again it was an agonizing wait before the demon screamed out and left. I was very puzzled, I must admit.

A few weeks later we were praying about something else entirely different and praying that everything hidden would be revealed by the Holy Spirit on a problem of deception we were encountering, when my friend said, "I am absolutely speechless". Then she gave a gasp. So did I. She had realized that she had made this pronouncement five or six times a week. It had become a spoken curse, a self-imposed curse over her life. She had always great difficulty in conversation with most people, lost for words even in simple situations. No wonder! She was regularly declaring, "I am absolutely speechless." There is power in our tongues. Read James 3:1-10. Do watch out for the unusual!

There are various foundation spirits, e.g. rejection and its often partner, a lying spirit. A lying spirit does not necessarily mean the person is a liar. It may mean that an occupying demon tells them lies about themselves. "Nobody likes you, you are ugly, a failure, you will never succeed, you have definitely got a disease", etc.

A lying spirit often goes hand in hand with an ugly spirit, spirit of unworthiness, spirit of guilt, spirit of the faceless one, shy spirit, etc.

Fear is another foundation spirit, and goes with a spirit of torment.

Please do not fear evil spirits. You have authority over them as it is written, *"Have no fear."* (2 Timothy 1:7: *For God hath not given us the spirit of fear; but of power, and of love, and of a sound mind.*)

When ministering I usually have a box of tissues

around and a small bowl. They are not obvious but just in case! I used to criticize others years ago – thinking "Jesus didn't have all that stuff"! However, I've realized that there is so much we do not know about Jesus ministering. Also we are not Jesus! We need great wisdom.

There is a washbasin in my consulting room, so that makes life easier, but we are not always able to minister in places with mod cons! Keep a small bottle of olive oil for anointing – and always keep your Bible open.

To me the open Bible is the sword of the Spirit out of its sheath. I like to stick Satan with an unsheathed sword.

Ministry of deliverance can be an exhausting, draining business, but it is the most rewarding thing I know to do for people. Sometimes it is so quick and there is such instant release. Faces change, stooped over people walk upright. My Father never ceases to amaze me. He's so clever. I'm always telling Him so too.

In my garden I'm constantly amazed. "Father, how did you make that butterfly? How did you get the perfume into those minute jasmine trumpets? That exquisite busy little jenny wren. How did you fashion her? That glorious splash of red on the bright green woodpecker. What made you decide to put it there?" I really enjoy bird watching, my garden is a bird sanctuary.

I once heard a preacher tell of a country man who died and came back from heaven. He told his friends who knew he loved the countryside. "You ain't seen nothing yet!" My, I cannot wait. Hurry up Lord. I'm praying you in!

Creation Voiced

I love to see the celandine gold,
Shining in the hedge,
To watch the willows' waving fronds,
Along the millstream's edge.
I love to see the dandelions and the clover mixed

In fields where works the tractor
With the harrow stoutly fixed.

I love to watch the ewes and lambs
Frisk in the fields so fair
Walk peacefully with my Father
for I can feel Him there,
To cry out to my Lord That I want to closer be,
The Lamb my worshipped and adored
Through whom I was set free.

The splendour of the kingcups,
Aglow in meadows moist,
Midst cow parsley and alkanet
Is all creation voiced.
My Lord I see your might
In each lush flower and tree,
I hear it in the songs of birds
Delightful harmony.

I am free of the future,
I am free of the past,
I'm living in the here and now,
With you my Lord at last.
I am free, I am free,
I am free as I can be!
Thank you dear Lord, my precious Lord,
Thank you for saving me.

Chapter 26

Being Under A Curse Explained

In the previous chapters of teaching I mention that being under a curse is one of the causes for hindrance to walking in deliverance. In fact I would say that this is the main reason why many Christians, who have sought deliverance from so many ministries prior to arriving at the Clinic, end up on our doorstep. I have long been studying the teaching of Derek Prince on the subject of curses and blessings and I make no apologies for that, so with me this is a priority.

Being set free from curse is a life-changing event for Christians who have struggled on often in the wake of everlasting prayer ministry and still not received the healings and blessings of the Lord which make rich. So they go on, not infrequently in guilt and self-condemnation because this fact of being under a curse has not been dealt with in Jesus' name.

Now in my teaching there is no time to elaborate on being under a curse. So I give a summary which suffices to cut people free. Then I lead them in a prayer.

At the time of writing this book, Derek Prince's book "Blessing or curse. You can choose", has been published. I am only two thirds through it having newly purchased a copy. To me it is very significant that Ruth and Derek Prince have suffered such a terrible attack on their physical health during the time it was being written. Derek says that the devil has been trying to kill Ruth during that period and that they have been involved in a serious spiritual warfare. Derek too has suffered serious health problems.

We are constantly told that the devil apportions his attention where most work is being done to advance the Kingdom by getting the gospel into all the world. Can anyone doubt that these two stalwarts for Jesus Christ must have been high on the list of the devil's priorities! I salute their endeavours and courage and fortitude in Jesus' name. They are a gift to the Body of Christ. May they increase in strength. I bless them in His name.

When I write this chapter I want to make it clear that these things I learned initially from Derek Prince Ministries. When I began I knew of no other sources of such teaching. Upon Derek's teaching was laid the foundation of my own deliverance ministry. Many wonderful teachers have blessed and helped me since – but had I not myself come out from under the curse in a big way due to this teaching all those years ago, I would not be writing this book now!

It would take a whole book to expand on cursings and blessings and that book is now available by Derek Prince, published by Word Books. I have no hesitation to say that it will set millions free and is of great importance to the Body of Christ.

It is also of great importance for non-believers, many of whom cannot receive Jesus because they are in fact under a curse. I have proved this over again in the hundreds I have now ministered to, many of them pastors and pastor's wives! It may seem astonishing but some have actually confessed to not being committed to our Lord although in the ministry!

How to Define Being Under a Curse.

In summary and in general terms it is like being under a dark shadow from the past. Life, however enjoyable, is always somehow clouded. Something seems to shut you out from the sunlight of God's blessing. You see others basking in it, but in spite of being obedient to God's Word you somehow just cannot make it.

Of course, you could be being disobedient as well, or involved in relationships which are not pleasing to the Lord. You may be a Christian gossip sowing bad seed about your fellow believers for example. You may not be receiving someone as a brother or sister in the Lord as you should.

If you are under a curse, your finances may be under a constant attack, or in spite of sufficiency in income you may never seem to have enough. Money seems to slip through your fingers as it were. Success may evade you in many areas, just as you felt you had made it, the rug was pulled from under your feet.

So much so that when all seemed to be going smoothly you were almost in expectation of things going wrong again and they did! That which you feared came upon you because you were under a curse!

You may not even in worldly terms be unsuccessful, but experience frustration in all you do, so that you are not able to embrace all the joys and knowing of God's provision and promises.

Reasons For Being Under a Curse.

1. Idolatry.

Idolatry is the prime cause of being under a curse and this includes the occult. God is very tough that we should not have any gods before Him and we know that He is indeed a jealous God. (Deuteronomy 5:6-9) We see how in verse 9 that there is punishment for these iniquities unto the third and fourth generation.

Involvement in the occult in general terms means that people have turned to other gods for information and help that they should be seeking from the one true God. Turning to, for example, those with demonic supernatural powers, mediums, newspaper horoscopes, etc.

False religions and societies like freemasonry are included in the occult. I have witnessed dramatic changes in the lives of relatives of Freemasons who are covered by the vile curses they make in their unholy rituals. There are so many books which detail these vile curses. Barry Smith's books "Warning", "Second Warning" and "Final Reminder" all contain tremendous insight and revelation on the Masonic degrees. Involved in freemasonry are astrological symbolism, kabalistic doctrine, ancient mysteries, occult symbols – many embroidered with Biblical names to make them sound Christian. The book "Second Warning" is imperative reading for those ensnared. Published by Smith Family Evangelism, distributed by Alpha and Omega Ministries, 13 Staplers Court, School Lane, Newport, Isle of Wight, PO30 2HT, England.

There is *no* way, if we believe the scriptures, that freemasonry can run alongside Christianity. I do not wish to give offence but it is an insult to Jesus Christ our Lord and Saviour to say that it does. Churches of Christian denominations are beginning at last to state that this is the case and a recent debate at the Temple Lodge London on Christianity versus Freemasonry revealed absolutely that this is the case for many thinking Christians. The verdict cannot be questioned, and the scriptures cannot be manipulated to accommodate this religion.

Derek Prince speaks on many teaching tapes of hundreds of people actually crippled emotionally and physically by ancestral involvement in Freemasonry. I too could document many such cases where the root was this particular curse. It scores high in my experience in resulting in mental breakdown, unemployment in families, suicide and the breakdown of marriage.

False religion and secret societies reject the unique place and function of the Lord Jesus by biblical standards. Anyone making a covenant with a false god as in secret societies is guilty of idolatry.

2. Not Honouring Father and Mother.

In Deuteronomy 5:16 we read that we should honour

our parents so that it will go well with us. Wrong attitudes to parents, failure to honour parents, puts us under a curse. Things will never go well for you if you disregard this commandment. It does not mean that you have to agree with them, but you must treat them with respect. As never before the present generation, under the curse of rebellion, disrespect and pay little or no attention to their parents. Children do their own thing and they are reaping a harvest of self-destruction and curse as a result. Watch for the single pierced ear in the rebellious child. You'll also find that he or she has many bondages. Nicotine, alcohol, sexual sin, loud music, blue videos, television viewing. What a plug-in drug that has become!

3. Injustice to the Weak or Oppressed.

A conspicuous example of this is abortion. There is nothing weaker that an unborn child. Procuring an abortion of a defenceless foetus is actually murder. Taking advantage of the weak and defenceless as in slavery and incest puts one under a curse. I have seen incredible freedom for people when the curse of incest is broken over their lives. They may not actually have been victims themselves. I certainly was never a victim of incest but it was quite definitely in my family line. When this ancestral curse was broken over my life I felt the release.

4. Anti-Semitism.

The Bible says that God told Abraham that He would bless those that blessed him and curse those that cursed him. (Genesis 12:3) That covenant promise passed to Isaac and Jacob and the following generations. People who curse the Jews are cursed. We prayed in Jerusalem to free two Palestinian Christians from the curse of anti-semitism. This resulted in freedom in other areas for them both, when they confessed and repented the iniquities of their forefathers concerning the Jews.

5. Self-Imposed Curse.

"I wish I was dead." "I am absolutely speechless." In an earlier chapter I wrote about the revelation of the mute spirit, and the lady who uttered several times a day, "I am absolutely speechless," inviting the demon back in continuously until it became a curse. Mary was a highly qualified, intelligent nurse. She always found conversation difficult. When she got home she knew quite clearly what she should have said, but was always lost for words. Just as some would say goodness gracious me, Mary said "I am absolutely speechless."

I told you how I used to say I wish I was dead, and indeed made attempts on my life. Have you ever said "I know I will not pass that exam." "I know I will forget to do such and such." "I know I will not succeed." "I am dying to go." "I am tickled to death."? Or have you ever said "I'm starving." Think carefully, you are putting a curse on yourself. Also, "I hate Christmas, I hate birthdays!"

Watch that tongue! *Out of the abundance of the heart the mouth speaketh!* (Matthew 12:34)

As you have seen I put many curses on myself, my arms and my legs.

There are especially strong curses spoken over us by those with relational authority, parents, husbands, even teachers. "You'll never make good!" are words that have albeit unintentionally blighted the lives of children.

One lady wrote to me that as her father escorted her up the aisle he pronounced "I'll give this marriage a year". That's how long it lasted!

Another lady who married a man when they were both young and he was already experiencing physical disability said, "I realise if we do marry I could end up pushing him in a wheelchair!" As a result they have arrived at the battleground of that very situation. This has all had to be confessed and repented, for although we do things in ignorance it does not weaken the curse. Hosea 4:6 says *"My people are destroyed for lack of knowledge"*.

I believe we can translate that as ignorance.

I have already told you to speak out Psalm 118:17 if you have ever declared that you did not want to live. Please do it boldly if you have to.

There are written curses too. I will again give you a personal example. Many years ago when I was married, I underwent minor surgery which went diabolically wrong. Until I was freed from a curse, all surgery I experienced was accompanied by a massive haemorrhage – which was of course a curse.

During the last simple operation, so minor that I came home the same day after a general anaesthetic, I bled profusely. The surgery was in winter. The place was like an abattoir and my former husband got bored with it all. It was my small son who was left to cater for all my needs as I soaked one bath towel after another and filled buckets with blood. Later this was confirmed to be arterial bleeding. I had consulted a doctor privately to have this simple surgery.

I was endlessly promised repair on the National Health, but like many N.H.S. promises it did not transpire. I saved up to pay for it myself and did not tell my G.P. that I had done so. I was afraid in those days to offend a doctor so did not call him when the stitch on the artery came adrift and the surgeon who operated and the doctor who referred me were both away abroad on long vacations!

I tried to handle it myself, my former husband moved upstairs out of our bedroom and I was left to cope with a small son who was indeed very capable but worried.

Unknown to me my former husband wrote on a card and stuck it at the kitchen window where neighbours or friends would call to see if I was alright. I didn't see it until nineteen weeks later. By this time I had bacteraemia and septicemia. My blood count was looking like leukaemia. The whole story was a nightmare and actually published in Doctor Magazine.

Doctors had ultimately to be called and I was in need of help, I can tell you.

As I wandered from my bedroom three months later I beheld a large card in the kitchen window. I turned it round. It was in my husband's handwriting and read:

"DO NOT KNOCK, RING OR BREATHE LOUDLY. MRS COLEMAN HAS RETIRED TO BED FOR THE WINTER AND LOOKS FORWARD TO SEEING YOU ALL IN THE SUMMER." Neighbours read it, the milkman saw it, callers went away not knowing what to do, just puzzled. And just as it was written I was in bed from February through the whole of Spring until Summer. I was two stone lighter and yes, "as white as death"! Don't tell anyone, "you are as white as death."

It was only when my team of girls ministered to me over a decade later that I realized I had been subject to both written and spoken curses.

I would like to say that I was able to forgive my husband from my heart and bless him in Jesus' name. This set me free from all the pain and anguish. I shall be writing about another case similar to mine later.

Likewise, as a child, although unhappy, I could sing like a lark. I was in choirs and operatic societies as a star as I grew up. I had a tonsillectomy at eleven with horrifying bleeding, and I had to be re-admitted and plugged to stop it. It was a long time before the doctors were successful and stemmed the flow. My voice dropped from soprano to alto before time and I did not like it. However I continued to sing and when I married I would sing away like a busy bee as I dusted and bustled around my new little home, not caring that through criticism of my voice by my spouse I was under the conviction that it was not a pleasing sound to him. I was so happy to be married. I had not had a home life as a child, and had lived in digs until I married, and here I was with my own little nest. I loved it. I sang and comments were made about my droning being flat or off key until I feared to sing in case I was. I lost confidence in singing at all. I started to suffer real throat problems which ended in a second tonsillectomy which I am told is unusual, as the first set of tonsils were properly curetted, not guillotined. I had great difficulty in singing again because of the fear of giving offence, until that very day I was driving myself to the surgical operation I have mentioned. It was in my car, my son was in the front seat. I forgot myself. I was nervous because of what usually happened to me – profuse bleeding after surgery! I was expecting it! So I started to sing from a current musical. I will never forget it because as I drove I felt that I was breaking through a long silence.

Suddenly my former husband shouted, "Stop that b----- dirge or I'll get out".

I shut up in shock but felt that I should protest. I was trying to cheer myself up. I had deliberately chosen not to sing a hymn, which I would have preferred and had chosen a musical he had enjoyed. To my comments that he should not speak to me like that in front of our son he replied,

"Well, you have got a voice like a f--- in a sewage pipe."

The car almost swerved off the road, my eyes smarted with tears. My whole mind became confused. What would my dear little boy think of his father speaking to me like that? I was a lady, I should not be subject to such verbal abuse. I had to grin and bear it but I underwent the anaesthetic in deep pain and sorrow. I felt that I was just a bore and a nuisance and I knew nothing about curses and demons in those days, but I would not have minded at that time not surviving the anaesthetic.

In actual fact, years later in 1985 I was being prepared for micro surgery on my inner ear at Bart's Hospital for a small tumour which had shown up on X ray. This had come about because I had endured eight perforated ear drums over about 4-5 years following ear infections, and I wanted to find out what the problem was. I was asked what other surgery I had undergone in my life. The lady houseman wrote it all down and enquired if there were any complications.

She was astonished when I regaled her with the ghastly history of my various operations. Even when I had my impacted wisdom teeth extracted at Guy's Hospital in London, I frightened all the commuters by hurrying across Waterloo station with a huge towel absolutely soaked in blood. Blood never dripped out of me, it always spurted! I recall as a girl of seventeen having a nosebleed in my former husband's (then fiancé) bathroom. The plug had been left in the handbasin and I was amazed to see how quickly it filled up! He was a tough Rugby player at the time and I believe quite keen on me. Because I was a long time he came to investigate. He opened the door and virtually fainted. He had to go and lie down. Endless cauteries of my nasal passages did not prevent this bleeding which was always profuse, almost violent!

The houseman at Bart's arranged for something rare on the N.H.S., a full spectrum haematology. She said surgery could not be considered without it. A blood platelet clotting problem was discovered due to Vitamin K deficiency. I was told that I would need to carry a card with me for the rest of my life. I was asked many questions on alcoholism and if there was haemophilia in my family. I have never drunk and all my replies had to be in the negative. Again, in the light of what I know today, with alcoholism in my ancestors, showing too in junior members now, maybe it was some sort of curse.

The wonderful part of this story is that prior to going into hospital my prayer group prayed against the tumour. The leader of my fellowship anointed me with a whole bottle of olive oil. Put his fingers in my ears and said "Out in the name of Jesus."

It was decided I should still go into hospital the next day, so I could testify.

Sure enough, praise God, the x-rays showed that the growth had gone and my hearing was restored. The surgeon was a Mason and was not too pleased when I witnessed that Jesus had healed me.

After the third blood test, while I had to keep going

back to the hospital to give further blood samples. I was reading a book entitled, "Where Eagles Soar", by Jamie Buckingham. This was in August. I was drawn to a passage on P.92. It read,

"In my blood flows the very nature of God. As a man grows into the very knowledge of God, as he is filled with the Holy Spirit, even his physical characteristics change. The life cells of his body take on the characteristics of the creator. Even the genes and chromosomes, those unchangeable and unalterable factors in the human body, can be controlled by the Holy Spirit."

That was a word in season. I received it in Jesus' name. The fourth blood test was clear. Again I testified to the haemotologist. But he could only declare that the initial tests, spaced weeks apart could have been faulty!! My case history, gory in the extreme, did not however support that viewpoint. He also added that should I ever need surgery again I should always ask my consultant to refer to the Haematology Department at Bart's Hospital, which to me illustrates that there is some degree of uncertainty in his mind!

However, there is none in mine and I declare that by His stripes I am healed! What glorious victory Christ has given us over the world, the flesh and the devil!

6. Being Humiliated

Humiliation can become a curse. Humiliation causes a spirit of shame to enter. That shame can be caused by
1. Something you have done.
2. Something you have had done to you.
3. Something your ancestors have done causing you shame.

1. For example, you may have been guilty in your past of extra marital sex, of cheating a friend who had helped you, of being involved in sexual deviations.
2. You may have been a victim of incest, or torment. The father of one lady was always tormenting her

by smacking her bottom when she had hardly been naughty and even in fun. When she wet her knickers as a small child he hung them on the front gate post for all to see. Children who are forced into naked photography. Sexual molestation – even falling short of intercourse, unhealthy fumbling and fondling. Betrayal by a loved one.

3. Someone in your family is in and out of prison, or is known to be the local drunk, or a bigamist. These are just a few illustrations.

Jesus changed that shame which comes with the curse of humiliation, on the Cross – for glory. For your shame you shall have glory. Who could have been more humiliated than our dear Lord, beaten, spat on, naked, mocked, cold, hungry and paraded through the streets to Calvary in that wretched condition? Do not take in the picture of a neat and tidy Jesus with the crown of thorns set on His head at a perfect angle and a tidy little loin cloth. The scriptures tell us that he was not recognizable as a man (Isaiah 52:14). He was a bleeding pulp by the time He was nailed to the cross. Any crucifix which depicts otherwise is an insult to the sacrifice He made for us.

When you understand that exchange you can be set free in His name and lift up your face without spot.

Job 11:15:

"*For then shalt thou lift up thy face without spot; yea, thou shalt be stedfast, and shalt not fear.*"

Job 22:26:

"*For then shalt thou have thy delight in the Almighty, and shalt lift up thy face unto God.*"

Do you lift your face up to God in praise and worship? If you cannot do this you have a problem. As I was writing this chapter I was on the sixth day of a seven day water fast for Israel, and for Britain to be set free of witchcraft which is mushrooming across our fair land.

The Spirit of the Lord revealed to me that Job 11:15-19 were the first scriptures I ever highlighted in my Bible.

This particular Bible was given to me on my forty fifth birthday. Prior to that I had never marked a Bible in any way. Since that time it has become a mass of colouring and marking. But as I read those words given to me in 1979, I can see that the Lord's promises to me in those verses have all come to pass, and as the realization is coming upon me as I write this, I can see too that when I had the revelation of having a spirit of humiliation, I returned in 1988 to the very spot where the spirit entered. It was outside a bungalow in Dorset. Two sisters went with me and came against this evil spirit which had blighted my life over twelve years that I could recall, and may indeed have been there long before. I shall always be grateful for their love and support.

I spewed this thing out of my mouth. At the time I still did not recognise that every curse was executed by a spirit, and I thank God for my brother, John Linden-Cook, who taught me that, and ministered to me against many spirits executing curses in my life. It was indeed a life-changing event and I never have looked back.

Looking at these verses of His promise

v15 I can raise my face to God and I only fear Him.

v16 I have forgotten my misery.

Even when I write these things to encourage you all, I promise you I have no pains, no regrets, no haunting memories.

v17 I certainly am always taken to be at least ten years younger than I am. My weight and measurement are the same as when I was twenty five. I have all my own teeth, my dark hair is not coloured in any way. I do not wear spectacles.

v18 I have found security. God has given me a beautiful home and Clinic and established me. I do sleep peacefully always.

v19 When I lie down at night, I never fear robbers and burglars as I used to when I was married and had a son in the house. I live in a quiet unlit lane and sleep confidently on the ground floor with the windows open, something I would never have dared to do in the past. I have had help and support from many godly men and women as never before in my life. God has put on my path some real stalwart backers, and godly men I can submit to with ease.

Above all I have Jesus as a husband, the Lord of hosts is his name (Isaiah 54:5). He has never once hurt me or abused me, but loved me constantly in spite of all the purging I needed. He has never rejected me and believe me He can do the same for you.

Again as I wrote this chapter I realized the endless times I had been given that scripture when ministering deliverance for victims of humiliation, whether it be for victims of incest, where betrayal had been a root cause, or any other specific reason. How grateful I am to God for those revelations. Praise His lovely name.

7. Barrenness – Failure to Reproduce

This is not only a reference to fertility – but in all things — FRUITFULNESS in all things.

Look at Deuteronomy 28 which contains 14 curses and 54 blessings.

The curses are for hearing God's word and disobeying (not hearkening to) it. The blessings are for obedience to God's word. Look at verse 11.

"And the Lord shall make thee plenteous in goods, in the fruit of thy body, and in the fruit of thy cattle, and in the fruit of thy ground, in the land which the Lord sware unto thy fathers to give thee." This list of blessings and curses are a study on their own. For example look particularly at verse 47, *"Because thou servedst not the Lord thy God with joyfulness, and with gladness of heart, for the abundance of all things."* We must thank God and acknowledge our blessings daily for all things. Tell God the Father daily how thankful you are, for your bed, your clothes, your food, your car, your friends, your animals, for His beautiful creation. He wants to be appreciated.

139

Chapter 27

How to Come Out From Under the Curse

We can make two lists of opposites for curses and blessings as follows:

(Reference and acknowledgement cassette on "Atonement" No. 4278 – Derek Prince Ministries. U.K.)

Blessings

1. Exhortation
2. Reproductiveness
3. Good Health
4. Prosperity and success
5. Victory
6. Head not tail (of any situation)
7. Above not beneath (of any situation)

Curses

1. Humiliation
2. Barreness (failure to reproduce) includes all female problems
3. Infirmity (including chronic or hereditary sickness)
4. Poverty and failure
5. Defeat
6. Tail not head (of any situation)
7. Beneath not above (of any situation)

The prayer below is the prayer I am currently using. I believe it is pretty comprehensive and since I began in 1985 to use it, I have altered it in the light of revelation, understanding and experience.

I am giving this prayer exactly as I give it when teaching. The spaces between the words are deliberate so that you too under the anointing can lead people to freedom with this prayer.

After the two Amens, I then as God's anointed representative, break the individual curses as the Holy Spirit has led at that point. In a gathering the Holy Spirit will reveal to you under the anointing the needs of individuals present. In other words you will receive a Word of Knowledge.

It is my personal experience that the Holy Spirit has taught me not to teach without fasting beforehand, usually three days. I always like to remember Esther's achievements with her three day fast, to encourage myself. I do not find fasting easy – but I do find it brings unsurpassed rewards. You can really make yourself available to God for intercession.

Should you be alone and unable to have anyone lead you in prayer, the latter is I feel preferable because of the seriousness of the nature of the curses. However, I appreciate that you may be isolated. If you are, simply continue at part 2, taking the authority yourself.

"In the name of Jesus Christ my Lord and Saviour, I take authority over the curse of rejection in my life and I break its power over me in His name" Go through each curse which the Holy Spirit has revealed to you personally and then breathe out each individual spirit which executes the curse. This may seem a lot to do but it's a thorough job done in His name!

If you have no-one to tell at the time that you are free, lift up your face without spot towards God and declare, " Father I believe that I am free from curse and I thank You, Jesus, for setting me free."

Again I really believe that you should try to fast at least twenty four hours and go before the throne of grace with prayer and supplication. Prepare with joy for this life changing event and give Him all the glory.

The Prayer

Remember You Are Praying to the Head of the Church the Lord Jesus Christ

"Lord Jesus Christ, . . . I believe that you are the Son of God, and the only way to God, . . . that you died on the cross for my sins . . . and rose again from the dead. . . . I renounce all my sins and I turn to you Lord Jesus . . . for mercy and forgiveness. . . . I believe that you do forgive me and from now on I want to live for you. . . . I want to hear your voice and obey. In order to receive your blessing Lord and to be released from any curse over my life, . . . first of all I confess any known or unknown sin . . . committed by me or my ancestors or those related to me. . . . (Confess your sins and any known ancestral sins. Do this audibly but quietly). Lord, I thank you. . . . I believe you have forgiven everything I have confessed . . . and, Lord, I say that I now forgive all other persons who ever harmed or wronged me. . . . I forgive them all now as I would have God forgive me . . . and I forgive myself. . . . In particular I forgive (name persons, speak out quietly). Furthermore, Lord, . . . I renounce any contact by myself or any related to me . . . with Satan or any occult power of any form . . . or any secret society.

Also, Lord . . . I commit myself to remove from my house and my person . . . any kind of occult objects . . . that honour Satan but dishonour Jesus Christ. . . . With your help, Lord, I will remove them all – and now Lord Jesus, . . . I thank you further . . . that on the cross . . . you were made a curse, that I might be redeemed from the curse . . . and receive the blessing, . . . and because of what you did for me on the cross . . . I now release myself . . . from every evil curse and every evil influence . . . and every dark shadow over me or my family from any source whatsoever. I release myself now in the name of Jesus. Amen. Amen.

Now, Lord Jesus, because of your people's prayer tonight I, as your anointed representative take the sword of the Spirit and I break in the name of Jesus any ancestral curse over them. I break in Jesus' name the curse of witchcraft, the curse of freemasonry, the curse of incest, the curse of poverty, the curse of sickness, the curse of accident proneness, the curse of rejection, the curse of the root of bitterness, the curse of rebellion, the curse of humiliation. I seal over the windows and doors of their memories from all past hurts and wrongdoing with the blood of Jesus.

In the name of Jesus I pronounce the forgiveness of sins for your ancestors and yourselves, and I say to you all in the name of Jesus, come out from under the curse and receive the blessing of the Lord which maketh rich. I pronounce in the name of Jesus that for your shame you shall have glory. Now praise the Lord, you are free from curses and ancestral curses. You are forgiven.

Now turn to someone and tell them " I believe that I am free from curses. Thank you Jesus for setting me free".

Notes

If leading others in this prayer you must be very sensitive to the fact that some people have a hundred people to forgive! Wait on the Lord, be certain they have adequate time. If people are struggling to remember names, get them to finalise with the words "And all the names I cannot remember, Lord. I know that you know them all." The names must be audible, though quietly spoken. There is power in the spoken word.

Chapter 28

Examples of Release From the Curse

The personal testimonies are of three ladies resulting from the 1988 and 1989 teach-in at the Christian Clinic for Environmental Medicine. They had been led in the prayer to be set free from curses following a teach-in, in such a manner as has been described in the previous pages.

Pamela

Following becoming a patient at the Christian Clinic for Environmental Medicine, Pamela was working for us as a receptionist and general helper. She was a very competent worker and she blossomed as she worked with us, seeing the Holy Spirit in action. In spite of her best efforts and improvement in physical health, she was still beset by Myalgia Encephalitis and multiple allergies and was like a limp rag. I had actually no idea of her complete background until she supplied this testimony for the book. I should remind readers that comments are made about her on the final page 256 of "Go and Do Likewise." This testimony is in her own words, and you may see the outworking of the curse in her life coming down through many generations.

Testimony

'I had been in poor health since early childhood, always feeling extremely tired, even after 11 hours sleep and getting frequent colds and viruses which always resulted in bronchitis. I lost my father when I was three years old

144

and at the age of 12 I lost my dear brother in a tragic accident on the very night he got engaged to be married. I couldn't get over my brother's death and the spirit of grief and mourning haunted me for 30 years.

Three years later my sister was very seriously injured in a car accident. Her spine was crushed and she had to endure several dangerous operations. Pain killers have almost destroyed both of her kidneys, and as no kidney transplant is possible she has had to have numerous major operations to cut away the nerves so that she will not feel any pain. She has had three perforated ulcers which have resulted in her having half her stomach removed. She also had nervous breakdowns during which time she stabbed herself, slashed her stomach with a dart and insisted that she had been raped, although there was never any evidence of that. She continually took accidental overdoses because she would forget that she had taken pain killers and so took some more. This was a terrible strain on my mother and I, and we had to watch my sister constantly. During this time my mother and I had to watch her brother die a long and painful death from a brain tumour.

When I was 18 I had to have a smallpox vaccination as I was going on holiday to Tunisia and I had a very severe reaction. I had a hole in my arm so large you could put your thumb in it, and had ugly red weals all over my body through the constant scratching. My eyes were so swollen I could not see properly. I was put on drugs for four years during which time I was not allowed to drive, which hit me hard as I had only passed my driving test six months previously. The drugs made me very ill and I lived in a continuous state of extreme exhaustion for the next 24 years.

My other brother's marriage broke up and one morning I found him in a coma covered with blood and vomit. He had been on medication for an ulcer and then went out and drank too much. Thankfully his recovery was quick and complete. Shortly afterwards I was attacked and sexually assaulted for the second time (the first time was when I was five years old). A few years after that my mother had a stroke which the doctors said had been brought on by worry and stress. Mercifully she had a good recovery and lived until the age of 71, when she died of cancer.

During this time I met and fell in love with Roger whom I met whilst working at Heathrow Airport. Six months later I had to leave my job as I found the strain of shift work and running a home more than I could cope with. The exhaustion was getting worse and in 1979 I had to give up work completely. I was getting more and more attacks of bronchitis and then had a severe attack of vertigo which lasted for six months.

Roger and I then took up dog showing and breeding as a hobby and after waiting several years for a really good show puppy we bought a beautiful black American Cocker. She was of excellent show quality and we drove hundreds of miles to championship shows spending hours on bathing and grooming and nearly always being rewarded with the coveted red rosette. She qualified for Crufts three times before she was out of puppy class and it was our dream to "take her to the top". However, I noticed that at each show my legs seemed to get weaker and weaker and when our puppy jumped up at me and knocked me to my knees, I knew the exhaustion was getting worse. It turned out that I had a severe allergy to dogs but it was not until I almost collapsed in the ring that we realised that we had no alternative but to let our dogs go. However, we could not bear to part with our "house dog" no matter how ill I was.

Eventually in April 1988 out of sheer desperation I looked in the telephone book and saw the telephone number for The Christian Clinic For Environmental Medicine. Although I did not attend Church I did believe in God and prayed regularly. I was diagnosed as having Candidosis and was assured that once I had got rid of this awful condition I would also be rid of the exhaustion.

Pearl asked me if I believed in Jesus and when I said I did she prayed for me to be delivered from the spirit of fear and grief and mourning. I have walked in constant fear since I was five years old and I have to confess that I did not believe that a prayer would release me from all the grief and fear that I had been enduring all those years. However, it did help but I was not completely set free, probably due to doubt and unbelief and more fears kept hidden. The Candidosis eventually went but the exhaustion continued and Pearl said that she believed I was suffering from M.E. also.

I had already come to this conclusion myself so it was of no great surprise to me, nevertheless it was very depressing as I thought I would never be rid of the exhaustion. Pearl said she could still see the spirit of grief and mourning and I had to admit that I was still grieving for my brother and also my mother. Pearl prayed again and I understood more about such deliverance. I was mightily set free there and then and although I still think about them all, the pain has gone.

On June 26th 1989 I went to the Woking Leisure Centre to see the Billy Graham Live Link and I was so filled with the Holy Spirit that I went forward and made my commitment to Christ. My life changed from that day on. Roger could not believe the difference in me when I got home, he said I was so bubbly and alive. My condition began to improve and four months later Roger bought me a car and I started driving again. In November I started work as a receptionist at the Clinic. I was drawn to Pearl because I knew with her help I could move forward in Christ instead of just standing still.

The first time I witnessed a patient's deliverance from fear I was delivered because I had the same spirit in me. Pearl prayed for me to receive the gift of tongues and I have spoken in tongues since that day. On March 17th 1990 Pearl held a teach-in on deliverance at the Clinic attended by many people. After hearing Pearl say how the scriptures tell of slaves being chained to the doorpost by holes in their ears and how it was wrong to use a cross as a lucky charm, I surrendered my earrings, my cross and chain, and also a cross I carried in my purse for good luck! I was then delivered once again from the spirit of fear, fear of accidents, fear of getting lost, fear of man and also the spirit of M.E., allergies and infirmity. I immediately lost my allergy to my dog which I have had for 8 years and only a few weeks before my doctor, a Christian, had told me that I needed to be set free from the spirit of infirmity, which Pearl knew nothing about until after my deliverance. She told me that she had ministered on a word of knowledge.

The following morning Roger noticed that I was not wearing my cross and chain and I very hesitantly told him I had surrendered it together with my gold earrings. To my surprise he said that I must do what I feel is right and the next day he took me out and bought me four pairs of clip-on earrings. Pearl told me after I had been set free on the teach-in night that God was going to reward my obedience in a special way. During lunch that day all Roger wanted to talk about was Jesus. My husband, Roger, although amazed at the changes in me, especially when I could go to supermarkets and travel on my own, was reluctant to share my keen interest in Jesus, and would not listen to tapes or even watch the video on Jackie Pullinger's work. He simply did not want to be involved.

However on the Sunday morning after the teach-in Roger listened intently to what I said about the teach-in and my deliverance, and then said that he needed deliverance also. Roger went to Church with me that evening and was so touched by God's presence that it brought tears to his eyes. On April 4th Roger had a mighty deliverance at the Clinic and afterwards he made a commitment to Christ. He said that he had seen the change in me, whatever it was, and he wanted it too! Since he has made a commitment he said that he has experienced a real inner peace and feels so relaxed.

I have seen Jesus at work through Pearl many times during ministry at the Clinic and I feel really priviledged to have been able to witness to it. I have the greatest admiration for Pearl, for her love of Jesus and for her ministry'.

Roger and Pamela both got baptised in the summer of 1990. We were loaned the baptistry of Courtenay Free Church by their precious minister and his wife, Michael and Mary Maughan. It was such an exciting time as three ladies in the gathering unexpectedly jumped into the pool! They were all from an Anglican Church in Shepperton, Middlesex, Julia, Sue and Sarah.

I never saw three girls so blessed. They were already committed Christians, but of course had not been immersed. The pure joy and radiance on their faces was a delight'.

Mary

Mary was the very intelligent nurse I mentioned before, delivered of the mute spirit which re-entered because she kept on confessing, "I am absolutely speechless!" I had known Mary, now my beloved secretary, since I first saw her looking me over in Sainsbury's supermarket in 1987. She asked me questions about the Clinic and I found her extremely difficult to converse with, mistrusting in disposition and very locked in.

Then a whole year later during my accident period I was in a local church where I saw the pastor praying for her and her husband David as they were leaving to go to Wolverhampton. I was sitting right at the back and afterwards was joined by the Pastor and a lady to pray for a girl I did not know. When Mary and David were being prayed for I saw clearly a plane tree leaf glimmering in the Spirit. I saw it three times. But because my ministry has been so misunderstood by local churches, I refrained from opening my mouth. I was disobedient.

When Mary made her exit, she passed by where I was sitting and I extended my hand and said:

"Mary, I am so sorry that you are leaving, just as I could have got to know you."

She glared at me and said:

"Yes, it is a pity you didn't come before, you might have helped my David." With that she swept out!

When I got home I started weeping. I could not stop. I really went into a travail. The telephone rang and a sister said:

"I just wondered if you were alright?"

I replied in the negative, explained the whole business of the plane tree leaf, and my regret at displaying the spirit of the fear of man. This sister then advised me to telephone Mary and David who were leaving on the Thursday. So I did just that.

Asking if a plane tree meant anything, Mary told me that they had one growing in a pot which they were growing to take with them as their house had few trees.

"Oh! I am so sorry," I replied, "I believe that I should minister to you."

Mary agreed and it was fixed immediately to take place before the Thursday. A team was hastily summoned. It was an incredible time and I had such an anointing, and was given incredible words of knowledge by the Holy Spirit. It began for Mary, who I did not expect to minister to, a long process of ministry in four sessions in two years and now she is absolutely transformed and has become one of my team. She has lost much weight, her face shines, she speaks clearly and is so easy to get on with. I love her dearly. She is beautiful.

She and David were victims of Church ignorance of the ministry of deliverance. They were judged, found guilty when in fact they were hurting dreadfully, bound to the hilt, bleeding and wounded. Mary was also a victim of ancestral incest and personal humiliation by her stepmother. Her testimony is as follows.

'After Pearl had explained to us the necessity for being free from any curse, ancestral or self-induced, we were led to pray the prayer for release from curses. As I was speaking out the words I began to feel a tremendous bubbling inside of me, like a great torrent coming from my abdomen up into my chest. As I finished saying the prayer my eyes filled with tears and I could feel a tremendous choking sensation in my throat.

A little later I received ministry from Pearl and the team and was delivered of a spirit of incest. As the words were spoken and I breathed out the demon I knew that was what it was. When the ministry had finished, although I felt tired, I began to feel elated and realised that I was beautiful to God.

Shortly after I arrived home, it was apparent that sexually I was a new woman. Always before I had felt in my subconcious that the sexual act was dirty. I knew in my head that in a normal happy marriage it should be "right", but in my heart I wrestled against feelings of uncleanness. My relationship with David my husband took on a new and wonderful dimension. I no longer felt dirty, just beautiful.

Needless to say, my husband noticed such a difference in me, telling me that cuddling was nicer and I was much softer in his arms, whereas before I had felt hard and unyielding. I just continue to praise God for the way He has turned things inside out for us, and delivered me from the curse and spirit of incest.

For 30 years or more I had a horrid habit, which I was unable to get out of. I "chewed" the inside of my mouth! The mucus membrane inside my mouth was continually macerated. After being cut off from curse, I stopped doing it for 2 days, but soon started again. I would do it almost subconsciously, and I tried time and again to stop myself. I had prayed about it, rebuked it, you name it, I had tried to get free. A few days later during time with the Holy Spirit, I realised I'd come to a crossroads. It was now or never! I became angry with Satan, I said, "Look here, I'm fed up with this bondage, I no longer want my body defiled in this way, it is the temple of the Holy Spirit. You know who you are, evil spirit that makes me do this, I tell you to get out in Jesus' name. I'm not having you in me!"

I breathed out very deeply, and then inhaled the Holy Spirit. I couldn't stop yawning for over half an hour. Ten months later I had not bitten my mouth. Praise His name. the mucus membrane in my mouth is smooth and healed and perfect. What wonderful freedom."

Dulcie's Testimony

"I had suffered from food and chemical allergies all my life. For most of that time I hadn't realised why I always felt so dreadfully tired and downright ill. The doctors couldn't find anything wrong with me, and therefore discounted me as lazy and neurotic. I was desolate – I felt no-one understood me even more. I then discovered alternative medicine which seemed to help. However I couldn't get to the root of the underlying cause.

By the time I heard about the Christian Clinic For Environmental Medicine I was absolutely desperate. When I told Pearl that I had tried Bach Flower Remedies, homoeopathy, yoga and meditation, reflexology and aromatherapy to name a few, she informed me that these areas were not in line with God's Word and teaching. I was shattered. My whole world, as I then knew it, was collapsing around me. I had always thought of myself as a Christian, yet like so many, I was walking in ignorance and darkness, not having seen the truth for lack of knowledge. In spite of the fact I thought I knew the Bible reasonably well. As Pearl shared with me and showed me the scriptures I realised I knew nothing and I was convinced on the spot as the truth of the Word shone out at me. I promptly renounced all these things, in spite of the fact it meant destroying hundreds of pounds worth of books and treatments, including money spent on training myself to become an alternative practitioner.

The Lord is good and sees what is in our hearts. After I had renounced these things and asked God's forgiveness Pearl laid hands on me and I was able to speak in tongues, something I had wanted to do for some time, yet there had been a block stopping me when people had prayed.

I therefore had to repent and confess before I was able to receive this precious gift from God. Within six months I was a different person. I seemed to have unlimited energy and I looked and felt alive for the first time ever.

Some time later, because of night work, I started to eat badly and I was getting a very bad addiction to foods, especially cakes and biscuits. My weight soared to two and a half stone overweight which made me very depressed. Pearl warned me about my pierced ears but I could not see what it had to do with overeating. I sought the Lord on this but it was two and a half years before I could bring myself to give them up. By this time I was wondering if I would ever receive my healing but I trusted the Lord that when the timing was right He would heal me. I continually searched myself to see if there "is any wrong thing in me".

Pearl spoke to me again about my pierced ears and reminded me that I was still in bondage to foods and that having one's ears pierced is a mutilation of the body. The word mutilation echoed around my mind and I knew instantly I had to give them up. The extraordinary thing is that at last I wanted to. I was convinced after the teaching, and couldn't wait to take my earrings out. Pearl prayed for me and I knew from that moment on I had received my total and complete healing. I gradually lost the excess weight of two and a half stone and I have experienced a deep and inner peace and freedom at the release from a bondage I had experienced for so much of my life. I praise the Lord for His patience with me, after all the years of searching to free myself. Only Jesus is the answer. When we surrender completely to Him and leave our burdens at the foot of the Cross, only then do we come into total freedom allowing the Holy Spirit to teach and guide us and drench us with rivers of living water. Then we can fulfil our true destiny as God our heavenly Father intended. To be the centre of God's will for me is the essence of peace. I should say that Pearl taught three times on the symbolic bondage of ear piercing before I was able to receive the result of it. When ears are pierced we are also in bondage to not wearing clip-ons, yet one can still wear both. Praise the Lord, His mercies are new every morning.

Roger and Pamela, Mary and Dulcie are all moving out powerfully in the ministry of deliverance. They all have the gift of visions and are exceptionally skilled counsellors. Gradually I have been able to leave them without supervision, to step back and rejoice in their embracing of the teaching and instruction of the Holy Spirit. They are — bless them — fruit truly abiding in the Vine.

Chapter 29

A Case of Unforgiveness

Melissa is not her real name. She was brought to me from Ireland by a relative who had been a patient at the Clinic. She was a very beautiful glowing lady, but full of deep despair. This is her story.

Four years previously she had married in her mid twenties. She married as a virgin and she and the husband she loved dearly enjoyed a wonderful six weeks together, then their sexual and embracing relationship stopped abruptly. Melissa turned completely away from her new husband, shunned his nakedness and refused absolutely to let him see her body.

An in-depth history revealed no incest, no repugnant sexual approach or requests from her spouse. She said she hated what she was doing to him and he protested that he would love her and support her even if he remained rejected. He was obviously a dear and patient man.

Melissa had travelled the length and breadth of North and South Ireland seeking help from psychiatrists and all manner of practitioners, spending £6,000!

One treatment was Gestalt psychotherapy which consists of beating your anger out on cushions. In my experience it makes the patient much worse. Certainly it is not a Christian treatment and of dubious benefit.

As is my usual practice (and she did suffer Candidosis), her allergies were sorted out. Candidosis, as I explained in my last book, can greatly affect both the brain cells and the libido.

Not to put pressure on Melissa we concentrated on

her physical health. I knew we only had her for six weeks before she had to leave her relatives and return home. All the time my assistant was attending to her physical needs, I was waiting on the Lord and addressing the Holy Spirit.

I felt to ask about her father, which she brushed off, but obviously disliked him. I was certain there was no incest or molestation – except for an incident as a child when she fought off two teenage boys with her friend in a car. She escaped and ran home but her father did not seem to take any action.

Upon her fifth visit she was miraculously free of Candidosis and all allergy. this was quick response but she was an eager, faithful patient, obedient to all our instructions. I confronted her. "Only one more visit Melissa – so tell me more about your father." I came straight to the point.

"I hate him", she responded revealing the first actual anger I had witnessed. Treatment for Candidosis always makes people very calm and relaxed so I knew this was an indicator of a deep problem. "Why do you hate him Melissa?" "Because of what he did to my mother" "Did he beat her?" "No, but he treated her like dirt, he always talked down to her, disregarded her opinions, criticised her and down-graded her in front of us and spoiled my childhood!"

There was a great deal of venom and hatred in her speech. I continued. "Melissa, this is the root cause of your marital problem. Subconsciously you are making your beloved husband pay for what your father did. You have to forgive him, because otherwise you will not be free of all this".

"I hate him and I'll never forgive him", she responded vehemently.

I explained to her that Jesus would set her free. She told me that she hadn't my faith and was only a lukewarm Christian. She went to Church but little else. I went through the scriptures about being lukewarm, and explained how the axe should be laid to the root of the tree, but she was adamant.

Time was running out for the consultation and I was in despair for the real agony she displayed. She too was aware of the time schedule. I advised her that her husband may indeed say now that he would be faithful to her without a sexual or touching relationship, but in six years time as he approached forty he could well panic and see his manhood waning. I told her that he may not leave her but could well take on a mistress or run the gauntlet of affairs.

I persuaded her to allow Rachel and I to lay hands on her and pray in the Holy Spirit for God's perfect will for her life. She agreed. We prayed in tongues and she departed.

As she entered the consulting room for her last visit I knew there was a melting, but she spoke out convincingly that there was no change.

"So what have you got to lose Melissa, by letting us lead you in a prayer to Jesus? You can tell Him that you are only praying in obedience to what we are asking and that you are doing it in his strength not your own".

I led her in the freedom from curse prayer. She spoke out words of forgiveness for her father and many spirits of resentment, anger, hatred and so on were breathed out. She inhaled the Holy Spirit and left.

It was almost a year later she wrote to me, that she fell into her husband's arms upon her return and they embarked on an instant honeymoon. He was delighted. She wrote that she felt 'new and whole for the first time in my life!'

The marriage continues, joyful and restored absolutely through the power of His name and the Holy Spirit. It is fruit abiding in the vine.

Chapter 30

Tom

Tom Folliard was 32 years of age when he came to the Clinic in 1985, totally debilitated with Crohn's disease which had been diagnosed in 1983 by the Central Middlesex Hospital.

He could not tolerate any food at all due to rectal haemorrhage and had been living on a daily sachet of soluble vitamins and water only by the time he reached us. He was also on Prednisolone, 5mg three times a day, Salazopyrin Alimentary and Sulphazaline 0.5 g. four twice daily.

To say that he was wretched and fearful because he was told that he had to live without actual food or lose his gut is to put it mildly. He was a driving instructor and because of constant visits to lavatories his livelihood was threatened. Tom was an Irish Catholic.

I am including his testimony in this book because it illustrates the overlapping of the spiritual and physical problems, and we do not always know which comes first unless it is really discerned. It shows too how seed was sown in Tom's life in a very quiet and undramatic way and how the Lord blessed him because he was grateful, obedient and recognised the function of the Holy Spirit in the Clinic. In 1985 the Lord did not have His rightful and absolute place in my life – but the Lord still knew my heart for the infirm and used me. He of course knew the end of my story from the beginning!

Tom had two little daughters and a very lovely gentle wife. To watch the family enjoying real food and worse still to smell it when he was existing on a sachet of vitamins and water was very unpleasant indeed.

So, written off by the medical profession, Tom arrived at the Clinic in a state of despair. He was bleeding at the time of his initial consultation.

We put him on about two dozen foods he was not allergic to and a vitamin and mineral support. He was allergic to the Vivonex HN vitamin and mineral sachet he had been prescribed. We wrote to the manufacturers to find out if the vitamin B content was yeast based. The manufacturers did not reply so I telephoned and the chemist could not tell us. I felt certain that it was yeast based and therefore exacerbated Tom's condition.

Tom would stabilize and then the bleeding would recur, pulling him down. Finally, led by the Holy Spirit, we were led to look at his wife. It was quite an eye opener. The letter below from his files dated 19.1.88 was sent to his consultant at the Central Middlesex Hospital. It too was unanswered.

Dear Dr. Silk,   19.1.88
This patient consulted us for Crohn's Disease and Ulcerative Colitis on 8.10.85. The patient was extremely distressed, having been informed by yourself that there was no further treatment to be offered.

He had been given Vivonex HN, a Vitamin and Mineral sachet, on which he had lived exclusively for one month.

He appeared unable to tolerate any foods without rectal haemorrhage. There was a history of haemorrhoids since 18 years of age; tonsillectomy as an infant and the usual childhood diseases, including chicken pox, measles and German measles.

The onset of the Crohn's, as diagnosed by yourselves, was February 1983. He was given Prednisolone 5 mg. 3xD. and Salazopyrin Alimentary. Also he received Sulphazaline 0.5 g. 4 2xD.

Upon examination, the patient was found to be suffering from Crohn's and multiple Food Allergies, including allergies to cabbage, parsnips, tomatoes, swedes, courgettes, pigs liver, plums, carrot, fructose, salt, Brazil and cashew nuts, onions, beetroot, brown rice, Indian tea, fresh yeast (Baker's yeast), and Brewer's yeast, bananas, cauliflower, Flora and Ryvita.

He was found to be deficient of Omega 3 and Omega 6 essential fatty acids and iodine. He stabilised on a grain-free, dairy-free diet and the afore-mentioned foods omitted.

He was seen by one of our Medical Consultants on 1.11.85 who confirmed our diagnosis of Crohn's and prescribed Becpharm Oral Nystatin 1 teas. 4xD. His condition continued to improve and he was put on intensive Vitamin and Mineral therapy.

He was also found to be very allergic to petroleum, which was a problem – since his occupation is that of a Driving Instructor.

Hair Analysis by the Biolab Medical Unit, London, showed malabsorption – and in particular deficiencies of zinc, chromium, selenium and magnesium on 18.4.86.

Treating this patient was not a simple matter. Many of his allergies came and went in rather a curious manner. He enjoyed long periods of good health and restored energy, with no reaction to yeast/mould tests. Bleeding per rectum would return intermittently, but he was much encouraged to continue with the regime because he was able to work properly and enjoy mealtimes with his family.

It occured to us, early in 1987, that his wife might well be cross-infecting him through sexual intercourse, which they enjoyed regularly. Mr. Folliard told us that his wife had, in fact, suffered from exhaustion and joint pain for about a year. We persuaded him to bring her for a Candidosis Test, which was carried out on 18.6.87.

Mrs. Mary Folliard was found to be a very serious case of Candidosis and there is no doubt that these two people were cross-infecting one another. Who had the disease first it is difficult to ascertain.

What we can say with certainty is that they are both absolutely fine. We have replanted the gut with Lactobacillus Acidophilus and have discharged both patients, who have been extremely well for over 4 months.

We are convinced that this situation has been dealt with absolutely and we are, of course, always available for them to be checked again in the Spring or Summer, if they so wish. They both understand the problems of the transference of this disease and how to maintain their strengthened immune system. It is very rare for a patient to be visiting the Clinic for such a long period. However, when cross-infection from a spouse is involved, a very determined application to the regime is essential.

They have both been excellent patients, and Mr. Folliard – who appeared to be on the point of death when he arrived at the Clinic – has been totally restored in every respect and looks to be only 20 years of age.

Mr. Folliard wanted us to share this success story – not only for his own sake, but for the sake of patients you are treating who are in the same desperate condition.

We do not have any failures in treating Crohn's or Ulcerative Colitis and many of our case histories have been published.

We trust this report will be of interest to the Hospital, and we shall forward a copy of this letter to Dr. C.N. Faith, Mr. Folliard's G.P. and Dr. James R. Witchalls, our senior Medical Adviser.

Yours sincerely,
Pearl A. Coleman
Principal.

Tom was discharged in 1987. It had been a long haul and a lot of 'detective' work, the detective being the Holy Spirit!

Tom was initially a very shy gentleman and we laid hands on him and prayed in the Holy Spirit over him many times. He also received deliverance from a spirit of fear.

He was extremely obedient and always did exactly as we asked him. He paid us a courtesy visit on 17.3.88 when he was feeling absolutely fine. I always get patients to score themselves out of ten for their health. When we asked Tom who arrived at the Clinic as nought out of ten, how he scored now he repeated. "Eleven out of ten!"

He was profuse in his thanks to me and each time I would tell him to thank Jesus and praise the Lord. He obeyed. Whenever he phones to tell us how well he is, he says "Praise the Lord!" I know he means it. We also explained to him how he should not pray to the Father through Mary. It was all explained very tenderly. Again he obeyed. I know that much seed was sown in Tom's heart regarding the Lord Jesus Christ and the Holy Spirit. I know he has been obedient to all we instructed him to do. He is also extremely grateful and has been very generous to us.

Recently he was just about to part with a large sum of money as an investment in selling a certain water filter as a secondary occupation and additional income.

I was able to caution him and give him documentation on this dubious product, preventing him from parting with his money. This was just in time! Another twenty four hours and the deal would have gone through.

Tom felt to ring me. We had not been in touch for ten months. He said to me. "Pearl, that was definitely the Lord". And so it was. I believe a reward and protection because of Tom's obedience.

So five years later Tom is still well and has no problems. I believe that what the Lord has begun in him, He will bring to completion for the Word's sake. Hallelujah!

Chapter 31

Wednesday's Child

I received this beautiful and encouraging letter in October 1990 from Linda Barnfield of Lancashire, concerning my first book "Go and Do Likewise".

Dear Pearl,

You have permission to put this testimony in your next book. I have prayed that the Holy Spirit will set free those who read it. I just thank God the timing was perfect, as at the time I was reading your book, "Go and Do Likewise", only a few weeks later I was heading off to Romania into the 'forgotten orphanages'. Your book really ministered to me and taught me so much. I was unable to put it down. As I was reading through the book I could feel God's anointing upon me and knew that the Lord was preparing me for what was to come during the next few weeks.

You spoke in one chapter of the Lord healing you of many hurts and curses, one of which was that you were born on a Wednesday, and you had been told as a child that 'Wednesday's child is full of woe'. I too was born on a Wednesday, and likewise told the same tale by relatives and friends. I do not think I got upset more than any other child, but when I did cry I was often told it was because I was a 'Wednesday's child'. I did not realise at that time that those words were going to have such a profound influence on my life in the years to come. Disappointment started to creep into my life, especially around the time of my birthdays. All sorts of disasters would happen. An overwhelming sense of despair and heaviness would come upon me. All this really seemed to happen in my early teenage years. My first marriage was full of disappointment and despair and sadly ended. Many things happened that were so painful, that just to carry on with life I had to blot these experiences out of my thoughts. Suicide was an ever present companion, and I spent most of my life just crying out for help. I married again and this too was full of despair and rejection, and now I had a terrible fear of rejection that seemed to grip hold of me. Physical beatings and words of discouragement pulled me even lower.

In 1977 I received Christ into my life, and straight away the Lord started a healing process. He has taught me so much and delivered me from many past hurts, and here I was one morning reading your book and the passage about 'Wednesday's child'. You wrote that you came before the Lord and He revealed to you how this curse had bound you, but as the Holy Spirit did His perfect work you were set free, and I too started to experience this curse being broken in my life. The Lord started to show me that although it was a curse on my life I had chosen to believe it and that near my birthdays disappointment was at hand. The chain needed to be broken, once and for ever. The Lord showed me Romania and said that on my next birthday my tears would not be for myself but I would use the tears on intercessory prayer for the forgotten people, children and babies in Romania. I knew that the curse was broken and I was now set free.

However I have come to learn that our enemy, Satan, does not readily give up if he thinks he still has a hold of us, especially when we may feel a little vulnerable. The night of my birthday, in Romania, I started to feel very ill. I was constantly sick and in a fever. I prayed in tongues most of the night holding on to God's promises in Isaiah 61:3 *"A garment of praise for the spirit of heaviness; that they might be called trees of righteousness, the planting of the Lord that He might be glorified!"* and

Proverbs 13:12 *"Hope deferred maketh the heart sick but when the desire cometh, it is a tree of life"*.

The heaviness had lifted by morning but I felt a little weak. My husband David prayed for me and off we set to the first orphanage. I knew that in my weakness God would show His strength.

I had the most special birthday I have ever had. What a privilege to spend my birthday sharing God's love with those precious children and babies, holding them, loving them and praying over them, sharing with them the greatest gift I have ever received, Jesus Christ and the Holy Spirit, to God be the glory in all I do.

Thank you, Pearl, for your openness and transparent life. You are so much of a blessing and an encouragement to both David and myself, Bless you and your ministry,

In Jesus' name,

Linda. xx

I praise God for Linda's very clear testimony. I have had five wonderful August 1st's now and intend to have many more. When I was talking about birthdays to my staff in the Clinic one day, they simply couldn't believe that I had never had a birthday cake. I told them that my birthday had never been an occasion to celebrate. Helen was so upset she went home and made me my first birthday cake. I had no idea she was to do such a thing. She left it under the back porch. I came out just in time to do battle with the local hedgehog and rescue it! Praise the Lord!

Chapter 32

Fruit Abiding in the Vine

Jane sat in front of me with her teenage son. He appeared to me to be suffering from severe exhaustion, because he could not get up in the morning and felt weak and shaky all the time. He had grown into a state of despair concerning his inability to keep up physically with his friends and was studying for 'O' level examinations.

He had formerly loved running but was unable to enjoy it or any other sport for that matter, due to fatigue. He was also under self-condemnation because nobody believed that there was anything wrong with him. Examination and history taking indicated faulty calcium metabolism, sodium toxicity, multi-vitamin and mineral deficiencies and allergies.

His mother was a timid little mouse of a lady. I felt nevertheless that she was a very concerned and sensible mother. They were very relieved when I was able to put a name to what was wrong. I was completely shot down when I asked them about God and Jesus, so I did not press the point. Everytime I saw Ian I wanted to call out a spirit of infirmity which is invariably in residence when the immune system is so undermined. He improved miraculously and developed such a confidence in me that I felt quite humbled. By the time he was discharged as fit as a fiddle I was quite 'in love' with him. He felt like a son, so warm and grateful as I hugged him goodbye. I will never forget that day. I looked into his face, it was absolutely radiant and shining. My heart fluttered. Here was real Holy Spirit material! We said goodbye and I found him popping up in my intercession.

Jane then booked in her dyslexic daughter. She arrived. She was fourteen and was quite the prettiest little girl I ever saw, with those bright eyes having the appearance of light behind them, so often a sign of need for deliverance. Eyes that look almost like lamps. But I have invited Jane to tell the story in her own words.

"I was aware that my family was not as well as it should be, so when I heard of 'The Clinic For Alternative Medicine'(as it was then called), I decided to give it a try.

My son went first because he had 'O' level exams in six months; he was always run-down and often had time off school because he did not feel well enough to go, nothing you could put a name to, just not well. Ian had high salt toxicity and was very deficient in vitamins and minerals. He went on the 'Stone Age Diet' and a vitamin and mineral programme and soon felt very well and went on to obtain five 'O' level and six CSE passes.

Sue was the next to visit the Clinic. She was dyslexic and very severely handicapped by this problem. She was then nearly fifteen and still had difficulty with writing, spelling and telling the time. Her sequencing was so bad she would sometimes go to bed at 9pm and wake about 11pm thinking it was morning. Her speech was very poor. She is an intelligent girl but was trapped inside herself. She went on the 'Stone Age Diet' and vitamin and mineral programme. She was proven to have Candidosis which was also treated. I was concerned about Sue's continual thumb-sucking. Her thumb was constantly in her mouth. She sucked it so hard that she had calluses where her teeth had bitten into it. By now we were beginning to realise that God is real and not just a fictitious prop for those who are weak and need something to believe in. I heard from Pearl in our early visits that thumb-sucking was a sign of rejection. I thought that if this was so, and was dealt with, it would help Sue in other ways also. Pearl said she would pray about it.

Before Sue's next visit I had an appointment myself

as I had now become a patient. I had Candidosis and was put on the low mould diet and oral Nystatin. It was very clear to Pearl that I had a spirit of fear. I couldn't stand on a chair because of my fear of heights, I worried about what to wear, how loud I should knock on doors (I always thought it was too loud or too soft). Also if we were in the cinema or on a boat I always worked out escape routes in case of the emergency I expected etc., etc. During this visit Pearl told me that my fear could be dealt with in Jesus' name. I was more than willing, it was such a hindrance in my life, however hard I tried to overcome it. This spirit of fear was called out and I was immediately changed. When I got home I stood on a chair and cleaned light fittings. My children encouraged me to close my eyes and jump and turn around which I did quite happily. I can now go up towers and walk along cliff tops with only the proper caution of holding young children's hands. The fear has gone! Praise the Lord!

At Sue's next visit Pearl had received from the Lord that Sue had a spirit of fear, a spirit of rejection and a spirit of dyslexia. We were delighted by these revelations and Sue was delivered of these spirits. Then the Holy Spirit said she had a thumb-sucking spirit which was also called out in Jesus' name. Sue knows she is now free of all these things and her progress at school improved greatly. She went on to achieve seven CSE passes including two grade two and three grade three. Sue arrived on this particular day of her deliverance wearing a key ring with a skull in a clawed hand. A horrible thing, but I thought it was harmless. Pearl explained to Sue that this was damaging her health and should be broken in the name of Jesus. She removed it, handed it over to Pearl who with great difficulty smashed it in Jesus' name.

My youngest daughter, Paula, came with us on this occasion. I was hoping that Pearl would have time to pray for her. She was terrified of insects. Even if a ladybird settled on her she would let out piercing screams.

Paula was delivered of her fear and that evening Ian took her into the garden and they allowed ants to crawl over their hands.

Sue then realised the importance of destroying things that were not pleasing to God. She took down a grotesque poster of the pop group 'Iron Maiden' and tore it up. As she did so, she felt coldness rush out of her bedroom and warmth and love rush in. She then disposed of other posters, records and books that she owned.

We had, at this time, been reading 'Nine O'clock in the Morning' by Dennis J. Bennett. I decided I wanted to give my life to the Lord. Sue and I discussed this and decided I should phone Pearl to ask her how to go about it. It was then that I said my first prayer. I had great difficulty getting through. I put the telephone down and prayed "Lord, if You want me to make this call I will get through; if I don't I will not try again". On the next attempt I succeeded.

Sue and I went with Pearl to 'Liberty Christian Fellowship' two weeks later and asked the Lord into our lives. The following Sunday Ian came too. He could see the joy we now had, (he said we hadn't stopped smiling). He gave his life to the Lord that day and joined the smilers. We had never known such joy. We then had hands laid on us to receive the gift of tongues, which Sue received immediately and Ian and I received within a few days.

The Lord soon led us to a local fellowship in Staines. Paula, aged seven, came with us. She really loved Jesus and wondered why we could pray in tongues and she couldn't. I told her we must ask Jesus. We quietly prayed together and I led her in prayer to invite Jesus into her life. We asked for the gift of tongues and she immediately started praying in the Spirit. Her joy was so great she was laughing, running and jumping all over the house. It can only have come from God.

Ian and Sue are both about to leave sixth form college and have seen several of their friends saved. Sue is going on to work with disabled people. She has helped both physically and mentally handicapped people, both children and adults, since she was thirteen. Ian is currently taking 'A' level exams and will be embarking on the career the Lord has planned for him although we don't know what it is yet. I don't know what the Lord has for me in the future but I praise Him and thank Him for all that He has taught me through my experience at His Clinic, for indeed it is His Clinic and has been dedicated to Him".

There is little to add to this testimony except Praise the Lord! Jane ultimately received many gifts, especially that of visions and blessed everyone who came into contact with her, before she moved on to pursue her own ministry away from the Clinic. God bless her and those precious children always. Since she wrote this testimony on 22.2.87 for my last book, they are all fruit abiding in the vine. Praise God for His mercies!

Chapter 33

Exorcism of Gypsy Dwelling Places

It transpired that Lana (not her real name) — a gypsy woman — had been unsuccessfully visiting a respectable Clinical Ecology unit, where she offloaded a great deal of money, and she had met a 'delightful kind lady' in the waiting area, also a 'patient'.

I immediately got a check in my spirit that she was not a patient but a decoy. The waiting area was full of the dejected sick, terrified of allergies to electric lights, afraid to sit on varnished chairs etc. It appears that this 'very neat, groomed lady' sought Lana out on many occasions, to share her despair that the treatment was 'doing her no good'.

"I am sure I could help you", said the obliging soul.

Dear me, I was already seeing the tea-cups, the friendly arm around her shoulder, the cardboard box in the corner for the non-obligatory fee! And so it proved.

"She was a very nice, kind woman, and she talked about God. She went to a sort of church", Lana told me.

"I bet she did", I announced. "Now look Lana, I am picking up the occult. I believe she was a medium, deliberately planted by Satan to lure the complaining and dissatisfied sick".

And so it was. I was told of gradual trips to this friendly lady's home some miles away. Then gradual return visits to Lana's caravans and the gypsy grandmother's bungalow. There all their dwelling places were daubed on every window with a cross and circle.

171

Now we were talking medium's talk. A medium will tell you that at night the cross glows and keeps Satan away! It does the very reverse, it advertises where Satan's tools have paid a visit!

Then the medium sprinkled salt all round the caravans and bungalow. Learning of the little daughter's infirmity since birth with a copious vaginal discharge, the woman told her to bath her child in the same salt! Then she turfed all the family out into the yard, grandfather, grandmother, mother, father, children, the lot. They were all very confused. Lana told me that the woman locked the bungalow doors and did something, and "was in there some time, but we didn't know why, she didn't tell us!"

You bet she didn't, one doesn't advertise witchcraft!

I was picking up such evil. I prayed for a while in the Holy Spirit. I was then informed that Lana felt peculiar because she had taken this medium the video of a very large family gypsy wedding – "so she could understand the family better". Dear God, we had to move fast. I told her that I needed to visit the caravan and bungalow site. I should add that these were no dirty gypsies but Romanies, with a splendid Mercedes car, and caravans decked in lace and brasses like a king's palace, spotlessly clean and in order.

I assembled two of my team at short notice, because the family were on the move, selling carpets for the next three months or so. Now the two I invited were very mature (in years) trainee members of my team. They had been eager and quick to learn. The wife had been delivered at the Clinic of Meniere's disease and lameness as a result of a stroke. This healing came following the deliverance of the spirit of grief and mourning and the binding up of a very broken heart in Jesus' name. She was widowed after six months of married life and alone for twenty-one years. Left with a baby boy after her husband had been killed in the war she had married again very happily, but the grief had not been dealt with. Then this dear son died early in life.

Well, this exquisite mature lady was set free and her disease and infirmity were dealt with and she had been testifying to the glory of God ever since. She also went from a size 18 to a size 10 in clothes and looked gorgeous. They were a born again Christian couple who had suffered agonies which their church, a large strong Spirit-filled church, had missed in the congregation of many hundreds. So Renie's ministry all began with forgiving her church elders.

I blessed this couple every time I set eyes on them, for indeed they blessed me and blessed many with their love, counselling and availability. They continued to grow and receive many gifts. What a merciful God!

We arrived on the site at about 2.30pm. Firstly we inspected the caravans and sat and talked. I wanted to suss out the children, a girl of about twelve and a boy of about fifteen. The boy absented himself following a quick introduction. The husband was a placid open minded man.

Frankly I did not feel very disturbed by the caravans, but the Holy Spirit was leading me in no uncertain manner to the bungalow. We exorcised both caravans dwelt in, and a third parked alongside, then proceeded across the yard to the demure, dolls-house-like bungalow.

It housed a walnut-like, wrinkled, nervous granny. The boy was peeping around corners of the bungalow and running away. He finally disappeared altogether. We entered through the kitchen door. Such a splendid kitchen, and my eyes fell on the polished brass crucifix. A typical gypsy treasure. "That'll have to go", I thought, but moved on, circulating through every room. The team moved in and out of the rooms separately from myself.

I was about to enter the last room when Ernest emerged with a look of horror on his face. The mother, grandmother, daughter, Renie and I went in, Ernest followed, clearly distressed. I picked up the same horror, it was very disturbing. I felt the same type of disturbance but less severe at the front door entrance which we had not used and was apparently mostly kept locked. As I had moved about I had exorcised all the rooms in Jesus' name, quickly and quietly.

Ernest started to pronounce in the nursery. "Ssh!" I told him. I wanted to discern.

My eyes had immediately fallen on the culprits but I wanted to check it out in the Holy Spirit. I was also drawn to the top of a wardrobe and a chest of drawers and under the play table. Ernest felt the same and here were housed copious copies of the magazine, about seventy-two in all, which goes with the occult and hideously dangerous game 'Dungeons and Dragons'. There were nasty cassettes and paperbacks with the usual spooky covers of snakes, hob goblins, weird eyes, monsters and tentacled creatures.

We put them all in a pile and surveyed the remaining contents of the nursery which included many soft toys and positively rows and rows of dolls, on window sills, in cots, and in doll's prams.

Frankly I have never seen so many dolls in one nursery. Clearly the small girl favoured dolls! All the time I was watching my trainees, because it is so vital to let them have their heads. Ernest was fairly groaning by now. The small girl was looking fearful lest her dolls join the pile to be destroyed.

She started to whimper. I just comforted her to be quiet and not to worry. The granny was muttering about the room always seeming evil.

"Well Ernest", I invited. "Is it the dolls? And what dolls?" The child clutched at her mother as Ernest pronounced, and we were in agreement. Renie also.

In one corner of the prams were the ugliest dolls I ever saw, twin dolls. One looked as though it had a cleft palate and hair lip, the other looked like a tormented spirit and its ears were pierced. I removed the dolls and set them all in a row, about twenty-two across the large wooden table. Ernest could not constrain himself. "They'll have to go", he deliberated unwisely.

The child screamed and grabbed the granny. Ernest tried to correct himself. "Only these two, dear, need to be destroyed". The child started to weep and wail. The granny and mother looked upset.

"Ssh Ernest", I said. Turning to the little girl I told her that the dolls would not be touched by us. I knelt on one knee before her and took her hand and looked into her eyes. I asked her about her vaginal thrush and how wretched she always felt with it. Clearly this was a case of Candidosis transferred in the birth canal from mother to infant at birth. Not uncommon at all, but we were in the presence of evil spirits and witchcraft over the child.

I talked to her about Jesus, His love for her and how she could be healed at once, and never need a salt bath again. She said salt baths had not helped anyway, but she would like to be well. Witches use salt a lot in rituals. Ernest and Renie were covering me in the Spirit as I continued to minister. We discussed the change in her mum since she had visited the Clinic. I explained tenderly that I was to break a curse over her. Fortunately she had not liked the lady visitor!

She was obedient to everything I asked her to do. The others stood back and once freed of the curse I called out the spirit of infirmity. She was slain in the Spirit and was instantly healed and has remained perfectly well almost five years.

I did not mention the dolls to the child, but I addressed those present, indicating the twin dolls.

I'll call the child, Jane. I told them that the dolls would all stay where they were but that the next week Jane would ask her mother to burn the twin dolls, because she was no longer in bondage to witchcraft. That was exactly what she did and six months later at the Clinic she allowed us to destroy her crucifix and she gave her life to Jesus.

The family are on the road but wherever they stop they find a fellowship. The seed has been sown, we have prayed harvesters on the paths they travel. The mother will minister, I have no doubt.

As we made to exit, in rolled a very drunken grandfather. He looked at me and shot out. The young boy appeared and disappeared with him. I looked at the walnut-looking granny. It was all there, years of slaving to an alcoholic husband. I laid hands and prayed, broke the curse over her life, got her to forgive him and called out the spirit of fear, rejection and exhaustion. I blessed her in Jesus' name and she allowed me to take the brass crucifix given to her on her wedding day by her mother. She told me that she had been waiting all her life for this ministry. Bless her!

The father took the huge pile of books and games to the bonfire and we were invited to the larger caravan for a cup of tea. I declined. We were not through yet. I was uneasy about the boy.

I told the girl to fetch her brother so we could say goodbye. It was not seven o'clock. The Holy Spirit forbade me to leave. The sister returned from the bungalow to the caravan. No, her brother would not come. The mother told the father to go and collect him.

"But I won't force him to come", he said as he departed.

He returned alone. I went to the bungalow, and entered by the kitchen door. The grandfather stood there menacing and swaying. I took authority over the demon of alcohol and the demon of nicotine. I bound them according to the authority in Matthew 18:18 and commanded Satan to loose his will to bring him into conviction and repentance of addiction.

This was all done very swiftly. I approached him boldly, and put my hand on his arm, looking him straight in the eyes. "I'm very pleased to meet you", I said, Covering myself all the while. "Where is the lad?" "He's gone to play with friends along the street". The granny appeared. I winked and departed. "A liar, too", I thought.

I returned to the caravan to join the other four and

relayed happenings. Ernest stood up to go. It was now almost eight o'clock.

"Dear God", I entreated. "Forget leaving, the Holy Spirit will not allow me to leave. Where is your faith? Pray! I'm not going until he comes to be prayed for. Why are you all flaking out on me? You pray too in the Spirit!", I told the mother. the little girl was swinging her legs happily in the sofa chair.

Well, to cut a long story short, the boy came, stubborn as a mule. I ministered to him and he gave his life to Jesus Christ and we all went home, Ernest and Renie to fish and chips. Very tired! I had visions of collecting some myself, but I got in and praised for a very long time. Praise the everlasting Lord! It's good to be on His Majesty's service.

Chapter 34

The Monkey Spirit

During my third visit to Penang in 1989 and the precious Full Gospel Assembly of Penang I was privileged to minister at Goshen. Goshen means plenty. It was a large house used for the rehabilitation of drug addicts and others with deep problems. As usual I arrived mid December and stayed until early January 1990.

Through a set of unforseen circumstances I was housed in an annexe adjoining the house with its own bathroom, and I was given a large counselling room next door.

The grounds were large and outside the corridor to my rooms I spied a chained monkey on a platform built into a clump of trees. I surveyed it curiously. The monkey was clearly extremely frustrated, prancing around in his limited circle. It looked to me as if the platform was some sort of built-in prayer place because it also housed some seats. And so it transpired.

I told the couples overseeing Goshen that this monkey in bondage, chained and restricted and obviously frustrated did not glorify the Lord in a Christian place. They agreed and had prayed for it to go. It appeared that the monkey belonged to a reformed drug pusher and addict Eddie. When I met Eddie, although quite definitely born again and committed to Jesus, he seemed very truculent and angry. He was slim and wiry in build and eloquent in speech. Initially he regarded me with not a little suspicion, but as I stayed on at Goshen he began to become more talkative. I felt that there was a great deal of repentance still needed in his life and a lot of rebellion still not dealt with. We became friends and he gave me his life story – which was typical of many young men in Malaysia – early experimentation with drugs, then a quick buck made from selling them to obtain more money for their own fix. Eddie had actually spent time in prison and was in his early thirties, although he looked no more than about twenty. His features bore a rather pinched look and his jaw had a very set and defiant appearance.

There was no doubt that he was attached to this monkey. I watched Eddie sitting in the tree with it. He would take it a banana or some treat, then he would sit down with it for a very long time. The little monkey, which I should say was extremely ferocious, would then meticulously groom his master.

Unaware that I was observing them from the window of my quarters, this curious activity continued at frequent intervals. I used to pray as I watched, and gradually I became aware that Eddie looked like the monkey. When the monkey was alone I would go out and talk to it as it frantically jumped up and down in its restricted space. It certainly did not like me and went to bite me upon several occasions, even after I fed it tit bits. "Don't do that to me, monkey!" I would tell it, "I'm going to get you out of here!"

Just before the new year we all gathered in the large community room where the organ was housed and services were held, for me to speak to them informally and take their various testimonies. It was a very exciting time and I was on my feet for some seven hours ministering deliverance to those gathered, in 90 degrees temperature and no fatigue at all! Praise the Lord!

The Lord gave me a word very early that morning to speak to them all about bondage, and chains being symbolic of bondage. I looked directly at Eddie and told him that so long as he kept that monkey on a chain, that he would not be free himself. That it was a Holy Spirit directive for him to loose the monkey into the jungle on New Year's day.

I knew how tough this was for Eddie. He had

experienced a great deal of rejection in his life and he was very attached to the monkey which was almost human and had become a real friend. He agreed to set the monkey free and came forward for ministry. Many spirits were dealt with following the freedom from curse prayer and he had spoken out repentance and forgiveness from his heart. There was a spirit of opium, a spirit of heroin, marijuana, rebellion, anger, resentment, pride, arrogance, rejection, lying spirits and many others. Then I was given a monkey spirit by the Holy Spirit.

As Eddie was slain in the Spirit I perceived an incredible change coming over his face. As I bent to anoint him with oil, there was only one word to describe his countenance. It was beautiful. Those next few days before I left, Eddie was a joy to be with. He was quite transformed, his whole demeanour was one of sensitivity to those around him and I was deeply touched by his gentleness as he assisted me in and out of the truck we shunted about in.

The staff and residents of Goshen all had ministry during my stay with them and the night before my departure they took me out to a lovely supper. I can only say that it was a memorable meal and such a happy time with these friendly open and generous-hearted brothers and sisters.

After the meal we all drove to the top of Pearl Hill, which afforded us a most spectacular view of star spangled Penang. The air was fragrant as they proudly showed me this precious beauty spot. Suddenly their excited Chinese and Malay chatter ceased. We all stood gazing out at the view. The presence of the Holy Spirit and the unity we felt in Christ Jesus was truly manifest as we stood there. A part of me did not wish to go home the next day.

Eddie had taken the monkey and released it into the jungle on the morning of January 1st 1990. We all prayed with them both before departure. We asked God to protect the monkey from destruction by other apes because it must have had a different scent to the wild creatures of the jungle due to being humanised in it's long contact with Eddie in captivity. Eddie did not weep or fuss – he knew the peace of obedience to the Word of the Lord and it blessed him.

But this was not the end of the story. In February 1990 I received the following letter from Eddie. I quote it exactly as it was written:

"Dear Pearl,

How are you there, I know God must doing wonderful things in your life. And God's love is in you. Praise the Lord! Sis Pearl I want to thank you for your love offering. I'm getting myself a new Bible and a watch. And I want to thank God for bring you to Goshen and in our lives, for you have already blessed us when you with us spiritually and physically. An encouragement to us all in Goshen. Pearl, I just share with you about the monkey. I believe God have used you to release me from this bondage. When I was young (5 or 6 years) I was attacked by a monkey. That time my parent gave me a red packet containing monkey hair which they believe I will never fear monkey again. Since then I have kept a few of them as pet. The monkey which I release before you left us it come back again after four days to a friends house in "Tanjong Bunga." She come back with a few of her wild friend and disturbed the house. So they called Raj to get the monkey. In Raj spirit he felt the monkey have to be destroyed. (My note. Raj was in charge of all the boys at Goshen.) And my friend's wife call him aside in the house and tell him the same thing which he has in his mind.

Intending not to let me know Raj hit it with an iron pipe so hard Raj think with that it will kill it instantly. But the monkey just broke loose even being chained by a big dog chain. On that day I was helping (YWAM) Crossroad with their luggage. Transporting it to place they stay. The last place is near my friend's place. So I just

181

drop in to use the phone to phone Raj that I'll be late that evening, and my friend tell me that I have to destroy the monkey myself and cut the soul ties. Then I will be total free from it and I'm now free "Praise the Lord!" Please to hold me in your prayer, patience, perseverance in Him and His words will hear clearly about going to "YWAM" (Youth With a Mission) in June or July. Thank God for fulfil my desire a Bible and a watch. God bless you in all things you do. Grant and fulfil your desire of your heart. God is good He has done me well

Praise the Lord! Love in Christ Jesus Eddie Fong."
Prov. 13:4

Oh, how I wept when I received that letter. The obedience of that dear brother to destroy the very thing he loved in order to be free to serve Jesus. Of course there was a demonic spirit resident in that creature which was why it returned and why it was so fierce and did not die under that hard blow from Raj, a very powerful man. Eddie's parents had put a monkey spell on him by giving him the sachet of monkey hair as a child.

Eddie has written to me several times. I have watched his progress with prayerful interest and it is exciting to realise that I shall be returning again this year to Penang for a reunion with them all. Praise the Lord, for His mercies are new every morning.

Returning to Penang in December 1990, I was delighted to find Eddie, brand new, exceptionally healthy, beautifully groomed, alive and energetic for the Lord. He had walked in the deliverance he had received and not looked back. Praise His name!

Chapter 35

Cutting the Umbilical Cord and Soul Tie

Heather, a vivacious and nervous young woman came to see me in 1986. She was then twenty two years of age. In 1983 she had been diagnosed as suffering anorexia nervosa, but since she had not menstruated for four years, I would imagine that she was in fact anorexic twelve months prior to the actual diagnosis.

The onset was clearly when, through her own choosing, she ended a relationship with a young man of whom she was extremely fond.

She had decided that since she was to be living away from home and beginning studies at university, meeting all manner of new friends, she did not want a tie on her home ground restricting her movements.

Heather was a member of a church and in her way a convicted believer, so she was extremely upset when she discovered that she had hurt her boyfriend to the extent that he became unable to eat for a short while and grew thin, causing concern to his friends. This compounded the guilt already felt by Heather and it was as though the spirit transferred to her in a curious way because of the soul tie between them. A soul tie is not always restricted to occurring between those who have had sexual intercourse. As in Heather's case it can result when two people have a very close attachment, which is binding, manipulating or even 'gooey'.

Following completion of her studies Heather did a little teaching and struggled through other various occupations which she had to give up. She lived at home with her mother, to whom she clung for love, understanding and protection to a very unnatural degree, not initially recognised by herself.

As with all anorexics Heather suffered severe candidosis, and I observed her progress for three months in cleaning up the gut and sorting out her allergies. I was at this time jotting down on her notes, matters I had hoped in due course to deal with, e.g. as follows: –

"Astrology, re-incarnation, yoga, fear of father, fear of man, spirit of persecution, unclean spirit through being fondled unwillingly under the water in a swimming pool etc. Clearly her parents did not get on at all well and her father owned a book by Dennis Wheatley entitled "The Devil and all his works."

Heather spoke of a black presence in her bedroom, like a dark cloud. She told us that she was terrified of it and one day as she was leaving the Clinic I confronted her with the revelation of the evil spirit world.

Her large eyes opened like deep chasms as she listened, she was very interested and although extremely fearful, anxious to co-operate. I took her very slowly through deliverance and ultimately she got born again and baptised in the Holy Spirit. Then her mother became a patient and she also got born again. The Wheatley book was destroyed.

On meeting the mother, a really stunning and gentle woman, I was able to discern that what we had here were a couple of witches! The mother was also a regular church-goer.

Gradually I got around to lending them Derek Prince's tape "Witchcraft, Public Enemy No. 1." I will let Heather tell the rest of her story in her own words.

"I had always had a very close relationship with my mother. Then in my teens and early twenties she became my friend and confidante. We did everything together, I even asked her to join me when I went out with my friends and she enjoyed it too. I suppose we were an inseparable pair – everyone commented on how close our relationship was, and how they wished they were so close to their daughters. I thought my mother and I were blessed to have such a good friendship but I was to find out that in fact it was not right. Because we were so much in tune, we cut my father out. We used to criticise and get at him, and worst of all, we tried to dominate him. At this time my parents were having marriage difficulties, and my mother confided in me. I sided with her and we both turned against my father. This had gone on a few years when I met Pearl, and she lent me some tapes on witchcraft and dominating women. We listened to these and both agreed that we had a dominating spirit and asked Pearl for deliverance. She said that we needed our umbilical cord cutting also, and did so in the name of Jesus. Initially I did not feel any different but over the next few days and weeks I noticed that I felt a freedom to be me, to grow and learn on my own, to be an independent person. My mother fell in love with my father again, and they are now like a honeymoon couple, cuddling on the sofa."

Heather's parents did indeed fall in love again and I glow inside when I see them together! Heather's mother blessed me for being the instrument in the restoration of what had been a marriage full of hatred and loathing. She said, "it's quite incredible, it is a totally new life".

Praise the Lord for His mercies! The father ultimately became a patient. He held a very high executive position in the city, and declared in the first instance: – "There is nothing wrong with me." As in common with all the initially reluctant dads or husbands who become patients, he had really come because he saw such a change in his family!

Well, we found about twenty things wrong and that rather jaded executive became so energetic and vibrant, that just as he is retiring I could easily score him as forty years old and very handsome with it!

Ultimately we also cut the soul tie between Heather

and her former boyfriend. She has enjoyed having periods now for some two years, developed physically and is altogether sold out for Jesus! It is great to look back and see this fruit abiding in the vine.

Chapter 36

The Sparrow and the Eagle

It was to be my last Sunday in Penang. Dr. Joy Seevaratnam and his family had departed to the mainland for a week's rest and family celebrations of a special event.

I confess that it was such a shock to find that Dr. Joy was not to be around during those last few days. It was not as if we were living in each others pockets all the time, for I was given much freedom to move out led by the Holy Spirit during my visits to Penang but it was always reassuring to have him nearby! I was in fact blessed by church helpers and given every assistance and facility for ministering.

The greatest blessing I have ever received from the Church in Penang and Dr. Joy and Elsie has been trust. In England where so much suspicion prevails concerning deliverance ministry, and one is regarded as being spiritually abnormal or even over the top, we often have to contend with much wounding from Church dignitaries, many of whom need deliverance themselves! The only comfort is that I am aware that I am not alone in my experiences.

A speaker from London Healing Mission, Andy Arbuthnot, said at a meeting I attended on healing at St. Saviour's Church, Brookwood on 27.10.90.

"Unless the power of the risen Christ is demonstrated in the Church, it will be the view of the vast majority, concerning the Church, that it is simply a harmless relic of a bygone age." "Amen, amen, amen to that," I cried at the time. Andy Arbuthnot repeated this statement several times at the onset of his address, and I wondered how many of those gathered in that Church had seen the power of the risen Christ demonstrated – had seen blind eyes opened, the lame getting out of wheelchairs, crooked limbs being made straight.

On my second visit to Penang I was taken to see an old man of about eighty at a place called Island Glades. He had been confined to bed for four years and moved downstairs so that he could be more easily nursed. He had a commode by his bed and a walking frame to steady him into his chair when his bed was changed. He could see nothing and his skin was white and flaky like hoar frost. His daughter was a retired nursing sister.

I got him to shout "son of David have mercy on me," for his sight, telling him to call it out really loudly as though he were desperate to receive. Then I said, "In the name of Jesus get up and walk".

He rose to his feet and walked. No, he did not dash about the room but he walked from one side to the other. He told me he could see shadows and forms. He was an old man of great faith. I told him. "Be it unto you according to your faith!" and I departed. I didn't hang around to see if God's Word worked!

Nobody told me until I visited him again in 1989 that the walking frame was dispensed with there and then, and he saw and walked from that day. He delighted in showing me how he could run up and down stairs, he described what I was wearing, the colours and my face. His skin was like satin, no more hoary flakes.

It is true to say that I prescribed some vitamins for him, but they do not normally get people out of wheelchairs! However, he still could not read.

As I prayed with him this time, the Lord revealed to me why his sight was not restored to read. He was still sleeping in the bed downstairs when he did not need to. Why? because the relative who had nursed him found it more convenient! The old man was more than willing to go upstairs, but this younger relative opposed it.

So there was a man healed and delivered but living

in the sitting room as though he was not – which did not glorify the Lord and in actual fact denied the reality and completeness of his restoration.

Boldness is indeed needed in our Churches. But when you say 'rise and walk', you have got to believe that Jesus is the same today, yesterday and forever!

Our churches need to be set free of deception and witchcraft if the Bride is to make herself ready for Jesus when He comes. I mourn that our churches do not teach on end-time priorities, nor on the fulfilling of the Great Commission. Where are the churches praying for the peace of Jerusalem?

So many churches are concerned with numbers and membership. Derek Prince says on a recent teaching tape that the Bible says 'make disciples', it says nothing about membership! What does church planting mean if it is only an increase in numbers?

The prayer that Jesus taught us says '*Thy Kingdom Come*'. How many Christians are actually praying the Kingdom in, crying out "Come Lord Jesus!"

As I walk around my Clinic I find myself chatting to Him constantly. "Well thank goodness you'll be here soon Jesus". Ask yourself. Is that ski-ing holiday, that retirement pension plan, the extension you are building onto your house or church, that longed for winter cruise, the parish supper, more important than our Lord's return? I digress!

So there I was snuggled up in bed at Goshen on the last Sunday of my stay in Penang, January 31st 1989. I was very tired, even exhausted by all the exciting things which had happened, many of which I am unable to relate.

During the night the monsoons came with an electrical storm. I thought as I lay there it was just as well that I had been delivered of the fear of storms a few years previously! I had always believed that I would be struck by lightning in the past. Now with lightning crackling all around the house, all the inside lights put out of action in the storm and my bedroom intermittently lit up by tremendous flashes of lightning I felt only the peace of the Lord. The rain fell in torrents. I got up and went to look into the courtyard. The poor monkey was very distressed. All sorts of creatures, particularly cats, seemed to be streaking about. The peals of thunder were absolutely deafening – and of course I lost a lot of sleep.

I thought I would miss the Sunday morning service and the storm provided an extra excuse! In Penang, church starts very early. Choir practice, intercession and an hour's teaching before the actual service!

As daylight dawned the rains ceased as suddenly as they had begun and the earth began to steam as the sun came scorching through with its customary brilliance. I paid a visit to my bathroom and returned to my bed to snooze. The Holy Spirit had other ideas. "Get up! Get up!", He said. I pleaded my cause. I told Him that I was certain that Dr. Joy wouldn't have minded. I moaned on but He repeated "Get up! Get up!"

There was no choice but to obey. I got up, wearily at first and then with some excitement I prepared myself for Church.

We praised and worshipped and the sermon began, given by a Church elder, Brother Albert Tan. It was on the glory of the Lord.

He opened with the scripture Habakkuk 2:14 *'For the earth shall be filled with the knowledge of the glory of the Lord, as the waters cover the sea'*.

He read Isaiah 41:18-20 concerning the sure promises of the Holy One of Israel. We were told that God's glory was going to be restored through each one of us, Christians touched by the Spirit of God, that rivers of living waters would flow out of us. We were asked what sort of vessels we had to be to carry the glory of God, that we needed to know how to carry His glory.

The reference back to Habakkuk in 2 Corinthians 4:6 was given us. *'For God who commanded the light to shine out of darkness, hath shined in our hearts, to give the light of the knowledge of the glory of God in the face of Jesus Christ!'*

Albert posed the question. "What is this knowledge of the glory of God? God caused His glory to come in a sweep of salvation of people carrying the Glory of God. 2 Corinthians 4:7 *'But we have this treasure in earthen vessels, that the excellency of the power may be of God, and not of us.'*

Albert continued, 'In our weakness the strength of God is made perfect. Get away from personalities and centre in on reliance of the Holy Spirit and looking into the face of Jesus.

What kind of vessel would we need to be?
1. As a Church.
2. As a people to carry the glory of God.

Matthew 6:13 :– *'And lead us not into temptation, but deliver us from evil: For thine is the Kingdom, and the power, and the glory, for ever. Amen'.*

Albert told us that we should be able to take the power of His glory to break demonic bondages and heal the sick.

We were instructed to turn to Ezekiel 1 concerning Ezekiel's vision of the four Cherubim with their four faces and four wings. The four faces were:
1. The face of a man.
2. The face of a lion.
3. The face of an ox.
4. The face of an eagle.

Albert taught us in this order. "The face of the lion represents the ministry of the authority of a King. The lion is King, the authority of a King ruling over principalities and powers. God is going to restore this authority to the Church, to bind forces and break demonic strongholds. The Kingly rôle; keep your eyes on it now and use the King's rod and sceptre.

Next we have the face of a man. In Luke we read that Jesus came as the Son of man. Jesus took upon Himself the face of a man, the face of compassion of

191

how to be moved for hurting people, the high priest who took our sins upon Himself. A human face, not only of authority, but of compassion. The Son of man came to seek and save that which is lost. God wants to restore to His Church compassion. Be ready to minister the grace and compassion of the Lord. Do we understand our rôle of compassion?

Then we have the face of the bull, the ox, the beast of burden, King of servanthood. True service comes from the heart. John 12:23-26. *"Jesus answered them, saying, The hour is come, that the Son of man should be glorified. Verily, verily, I say unto you, Except a grain of wheat fall into the ground and die, it abideth alone: but if it die, it bringeth forth much fruit. He that loveth his life shall lose it; and he that hateth his life in this world shall keep it unto life eternal. If any man serve me, let him follow me, and where I am, there shall also my servant be: if any man serve me, him will my Father honour"*. The servant attitude is what Jesus bore. He was humbled even unto death. True servanthood! We like to serve where we are seen. If anyone serves me tell him to follow me. It's not where I want to be. When we yield ourselves to His will the glory of the Lord awaits us. Do not consider the cost.

The next is the face of the eagle. The eagle is king. When the storm comes he goes against it, he flies above it where the sun is. He overcomes. 1 John 5:4. *"For whatsoever is born of God overcometh the world; and this is the victory that overcometh the world, even our faith"*. Say, 'I am going to defeat the devil, I will not give him any ground.' Are you taking it from the devil? Arise, speak the word of faith. Stretch forth your wings, break through the clouds. Faith is not faith until it inherits the promise. Faith endures to the end and receives the promise.

To carry the glory of God we need to have the face of the eagle, to be people who break through. The Church needs to be aware of its kingly rôle, aware of compassion

192

and how to be the servant and how to overcome. We are in the centre. A live coal burning within our hearts is the zeal of the Lord consuming you. Be violent for the Kingdom of God.

Glory is the outward manifestation of the character of God, which is holiness. He says, "I will put my Spirit of holiness within you. True holiness!"

The Bible says that the Spirit was in the wheels of the Cherubim (Ezekiel 1:20) The wheels were under the control of the Spirit of God, so be sensitive to the Holy Spirit, obedient to what God is saying. Grace is the ability to earn you the glory of God. Ezekiel was given a vision of the Cherubim which carried the glory of the Lord'.

The aforesaid is taken from my notes on the sermon and from the tape. Readers should remember that the speaker is Chinese.

Whenever I heard Albert preach I always likened him to a human dynamo and he would jump up and down excitedly as he praised, worshipped and taught. The Lord bless him!

Albert concluded that people had to make a decision whether they were going to continue to wallow in their own mire and be like sparrows hopping around on the ground or rise up like the eagle, soaring heavenwards against the storm above the clouds.

My stomach somersaulted as he spoke these words, the echo of the vision I received some four days earlier of the sparrow and the bronze eagle. I started to shake in my gut and tremble all over.

I recalled some ten years previously hearing Ian Andrews say that if one felt one had something from God one would not feel cocky about it but tremulous with heart thumping and gut churning. I was experiencing all these symptoms. I glanced across at the church prophet. He nodded. I crossed the aisle to speak to him and he urged me to go up front and confirm the Word with the vision the Lord had given me when praying for about an hour in the Spirit with a sister to whom I had ministered deliverance. I was getting nothing but remembering Luke 18:1 I pressed on in and suddenly I saw to the left of my vision a small house sparrow hopping about on the ground. Then to the right I saw a large bronze eagle perched ready to take off. I continued to pray and over this vision I saw tears, but the tears were made of wood. I could clearly see the grain in them.

As I was looking at those tears, the eagle suddenly took off soaring heavenwards. I knew that the vision was for the church. I recalled hearing in the church earlier in my visit, reference to gold and silver eagles. I was very curious about this and asked Dr. Joy Seevaratnam at lunch after church what this meant. The golden eagles were the over seventies and the silver eagles the over forties in the church. It was an affectionate reference to these groupings of ages. So I said to Dr. Joy the bronze eagles must be the younger men and women. He agreed. He also explained that the wooden tears were the tears of self-pity in the church. "Hmm!" I thought, I would have to pray that all through.

John had been at the table that time when I had shared with Dr. Joy. I was so nervous I asked if he would come up with me. It is a vast congregation of some thousand people and was not an easy matter for me. John was insistent and the Lord definite, so I obeyed. I also feared to disobey the Lord.

Before Albert handed me the microphone he told the congregation that before he asked our sister to share he should say that earlier that morning before the service he had felt in his spirit that Sister Pearl would confirm the Word.

I was so delighted and blessed and this gave me the confidence to bring the vision boldly. God was wanting this precious people to stop wallowing in self-pity and to rise above it like eagles flying into the storm as overcomers.

As I spoke I was never more certain that I had heard from God. A total peace and joy descended upon me. I was built up in the Spirit.

What is more, at the conclusion of that service, and he told me totally unexpectedly, I was prohesied over by John. I have had some powerful prophecies prayed over me in my time. I have even come under the condemnation of a local pastor for that. Here in one powerful prophecy was the absolute confirmation of all the others. I could not believe that I had been deceived. I knew it was from God. What is more it contained an ultimatum if I did not obey.

I came home and shared with the team who confirmed what had been said and prayed with me and encouraged me not to falter, whatever criticism I received from men! I knew, too, that I had come to a place in my life, where Jesus had absolute supremacy over my own tiny will. He reigned in me. He was sovereign in my life. I cared only to be His obedient servant. I was finally set free of self-doubt!

So there in Penang through that church, its love, trust and encouragement, I turned away from any calling the world had upon my time and I set my face like a flint towards obedience at any price. For the first time I ceased to regard the ministry as something God was forcing me to do, and saw it as a privilege and honour to serve the oppressed and the Body of Christ in this way.

I was so blessed. Fruit continued to pour in as graciously people responded to my book "Go And Do Likewise". The Lord in this response confirmed the dire need for captives, particularly in the churches, to be set free, and the scarcity of folks willing to undertake this unpopular and misunderstood ministry. I have been blessed by the humility of many exposing very terrible sores. I too have been able to witness the team members moving out, many blessing their own local churches. I have continued with the team to teach this ministry to others, investing in their precious lives. Our numbers were added to and the Lord spoke to many of us concerning praying for the peace of Jerusalem, and of intercession for Israel. I was told that the ministry came second to this requirement. It has not been easy to adjust because of the increased demand for ministry, but I am tackling it with zeal.

I said that my face was set like flint towards obedience. I think it would be true to say that my face is set towards Jerusalem, for the apple of His eye is constantly occupying my thoughts and prayer time.

We need to bind the spirit of Anti-Christ over Israel and release the spirit of Christianity and the Lord Jesus Christ in its place. I believe that when intercessors do this, strongholds will be broken allowing the increase of Jewish believers. Are British readers aware that there are now more Moslems in Britain that practising Christians, that we can no longer be called a Christian country?

Chapter 37

The Grace of Yielding

I made plans to visit Jerusalem in May/June 1990 for the Shavuot Celebration. This was not until demonic intervention had prevented my going earlier, but as it transpired the Lord changed the curse of that upset into a blessing, because I enjoyed both my visit and incredible teaching as well, not only at the Shavuot Conference but from the very anointed guide provided by Shoresh Tours.

Of course I have heard of Christian visitors to Israel being overcome and moved treading where our Lord trod, but truly I was not expecting that beautiful Holy Land to have such an intangible effect on my spirit. Although I was extremely tired from early rising for prayer, lectures and much travelling, I found myself unable to sleep until I had wept on my face for Jerusalem.

I had received a word to go and stand on the Mount of Olives and intercede, but when we arrived, because of the stirrings and shootings around Jerusalem and around her borders there seemed to be no way that I could get there.

However the Lord's provision was evident once more, and through meeting someone at the conference, Angela and I were able to go and pray in the garden of a house on the mountain slopes for as long as we wished.

My arrival in Jerusalem was incredible for another reason. I am not in the habit of absenting myself from the Clinic more than once a year, for financial reasons. I had only returned from Penang early January 1990 – so it was unthinkable I should be making plans to depart elsewhere.

I had not been home for very long and I was treating myself to a rare languishing in the bath. I was playing a tape by Derek Prince entitled "The Grace of Yielding". The question seemingly being posed was did we have any idols? Were we guilty of the sin of idolatry? I lay there contentedly, speaking aloud to the Lord. "Well, Lord, I'm sure I've given up all my idols and this aspect of obedience has been dealt with in my life."

Then Derek started elaborating on what idols could be, like a pension plan or insurance scheme, a denominational affiliation or taking Daddy along with us. Maybe it was something God had given us, a ministry or a gift, some achievement, or a person.

He spoke about faith being matured by steps of obedience, and how even if God had given us something He may have blessed it, but wanted it back. In which case he continued, we should be prepared to lay it on the altar or miss God's blessing. If you thought something was your baby, rather than see it die, you should give it away. He said that many servants of the Lord, through holding on to their Isaac, found that it was all they were left with – and how if you surrendered your Isaac God would be responsible.

There were so many pearls of wisdom which seemed to plop in the water around me as I lay soaking. I was made to realise in a much deeper way the faith of Abraham, inasmuch as his miracle child, God's supernatural gift, was also Abraham's promised inheritance – yet when God required him back as a burnt sacrifice Abraham immediately obeyed. He did not hang around waiting for God to change His mind, or beg Him to do so, but made ready at once for the journey to Mount Moriah – believing that God was able to raise Isaac from the dead.

Derek talked about the yielding spirit and its opposite, the grabbing spirit, that only yielding brings the inheritance, that faith is not a static condition but progressive. The mark that separates is the Spirit of Christ

– and the fact that our strength is the ability to bear the infirmities of the weak.

God had given me that scripture, Romans 15:1, so often, and yet I received all these well-known and formerly pondered-on scriptures afresh into my spirit. That is what is so wonderful about the Word of God. Revelations from it are continuously opening up as we grow spiritually. In order to receive them in a new way we are ourselves opened up!

I recalled, as I lay there, the real joy when I found that I could teach the ministry of deliverance to others and step back and let them do it, investing in the lives of others by sharing what God has given me. In fact I can truly say that I came to enjoy the teaching more than casting out demons myself and that I feel the teaching is really more important.

I was checking out in my mind and in prayer that when I laid the ministry down in January 1988 on my way home from Penang, I felt such a complete peace in so doing – and the Lord in an incredible way then gave me the air stewardess and chief steward to minister to – and they both got delivered of the spirit of nicotine high above the seas. I then asked for a third confirmation and got it through ministry at Brussels airport.

I recognised that same sort of peace coming over me as the tape played on and I knew that I was receiving something into my spirit. At that point I stopped the tape and simply lay very still in the bath. I was listening to God with my spiritual ears. I was also listing the other things I had laid down for the Lord, dancing, sports clubs, socialising in the worldly sense, eye make-up, certain types of clothes and jewellery, television, although that was never a problem or a sacrifice, I simply chose not to keep it on after the news! My husband, my son, the man I loved, certain worldly friends and certain worldly places, London theatres, concerts, quaint country public houses. I never drank or smoked, but I just felt that I should not use them for snack meals when we were walking, only as a last resort. Also they are invariably full of demons and in one sense I like to be off-duty sometimes!

Seriously, I am not a paragon of virtue, but I do believe that handmaidens of the Lord must beware where they set their feet and 1 Corinthians 5:9-11 applies. I like the Amplified Version best. *"9. I wrote to you in my (previous) letter not to (associate closely and habitually) with unchaste (impure) people; 10. Not (meaning of course that you must) altogether shun the immoral people of this world, or the greedy graspers and cheats and thieves or idolaters, since otherwise you need to get out of the world of human society altogether! 11. But now I write to you not to associate with anyone who bears the name of (Christian) brother, if he is known to be guilty of immorality or greed, or is an idolater – that is, whose soul is devoted to any object that usurps the place of God – or (is) a person with a foul tongue (railing, abusing, reviling, slandering), or is a drunkard, or a swindler, robber. (No) you must not so much eat with such a person."*

I fasted my newspapers, then I found I only needed two a week – because the news was in the Bible anyway! I used to be in bondage and pressurised to read every medical journal and keep abreast of every new drug and its side effects. When I released this to the Lord, He always provided me information as and when I needed it.

As I dwelt on the memory of not having to soak up all those journals, and a lot of them are weekly, I felt such a reminder of the release I enjoyed at the time. General Practioner, Doctor, Pulse, Update, The Physician, B.M.J., Lancet, The Practitioner and so on. What a bondage!

Now this was a sequence of events as I let my thoughts wander over the past relinquishments. There had been a lot of pride in keeping up with the journals, because many doctors didn't. Having various bits of medical equipment in my consulting room just in case – but with the Holy Spirit one does not need them really!

The Christian Clinic For Environmental Medicine is, of course, definitely the Lord's and I am the steward of His provision. I thought — **His Provision**. My mind dwelt on those two words. I didn't think I was too happy about what I was receiving.

Yes, God gave me the Clinic and prospered it and beautified it, and I had taken care that it glorified Him. At the same time it also became my income for light, heat, power, telephone bills, mortgage, insurances, car, food, petrol, etc., etc.

It was revealed to me that this in itself had become a bondage. It had to be clinically ecologically cleaned and opened on certain days. I had to be available to patients seven days and nights a week – because I offered a personal service to many sick, desperate and emotionally or physically lame people. I could not take holidays in case I was needed.

I became horribly convicted of much. The bath water was now stone cold. I was beginning to feel a little chilled myself as my self-examination continued.

Like all clinics and firms we had suffered the effects of recession. Things had been less easy financially during the last year and we had economised where possible. Lurking in the back of my mind was the mortgage and constant repairs on the property. I became convicted in my spirit with some considerable gut churning that God wanted the Clinic back and I was to make myself redundant!

I topped up the bath with hot water and switched on the tape. I thought I should listen to the end before I made a decision – and in order to make that decision I had to override the question uppermost in my mind. How should I live? Did I trust God enough?

Dear me! It was not a very affluent time to make such a decision. But is it ever? As the tape concluded I was climbing out of the bath, face down on the floor in all my nakedness – giving God the Clinic. And He took it!

No new patients came, work fell off with extraordinary rapidity. I never really imagined God would answer so quickly. Then I was comforted by recalling what happened to Dr. Joy when he said "OK Lord, whatever is Your will" – and three days later he was out of a job!!

So bit by bit as the telephone became silent in a once busy Clinic I had to release various securities, I cashed life insurances, I expended nest eggs of one sort or another. There were not even any Clinic enquiries! I sold bits and pieces and God watched my every action, I know.

The more I released the more peace I felt. I was not in any doubt about what God was saying. I spent more time with Him, I was able to pray for more deliverance, enjoy the Clinic as my home and garden in a very peaceful and contented way. I stopped striving to keep things together for the first time in my life. My staff of five became four, then three, then two, then one. I was doing about half a day's work with patients where treatment was ongoing or not yet concluded.

Then one week there was nothing. I did not have to fight the fear that I expected to. I decided that I would really enjoy this week, not having to set up the Clinic. What is more I went shopping! I really treated myself to some new and fashionable clothes, some perfume and one or two other items. I took myself out to lunch. I was demonstrating to my Father that I did not believe I was spending my reserves, my last penny. Then to top it all I booked in faith for Jerusalem.

I returned on June 1st – my book was published on May 28th. Authors commit themselves to purchasing so many books. My quota were lined up in the hall. Naturally I was excited – and the moment I thought, "Ah! This will be an income," I confessed and repented it.

"No, Father, you are my Jehovah Jireh – and You have supplied all my needs according to Your riches in glory. I trust You absolutely for the future. I'll not put

my trust in chariots or horses or books – only You."
Then I gave 200 books away!

This released such a blessing which included the first persons, a couple I had ministered to from a local church in 1988, being led by the Spirit to tithe to the Clinic.

Then the telephone started buzzing and a harvest of new patients started to come in. I didn't know really what to do, so I gave the Clinic to a sister Rachel who had worked faithfully as my assistant for two years. Rachel is a former YWAM missionary. Her family have spent their lives on the mission field. She is absolutely brilliant and has quite overtaken me in many clinical areas.

But somehow Rachel did not receive in her spirit to take the job on. She also runs a kindergarten school with her husband in Kent.

So back to the closet! The Lord revealed that He had given the Clinic back to me, that in particular it was for Christians, although not exclusively. So now I did not have enough staff – everything had to be geared up again! But the Lord said that this was not the case. That I was to see patients one day a week only, one day packed tight, but that the remainder of the time was to be given to seeking His face, to studying the Word, to pray for Israel and set the captives free. I was to be available to Him, to watch and to pray.

There has been a lot of adjusting to do in my life — but basically I have let go to let God and I am peaceful and happy. The joy of the Lord is my strength. God has made me, through obedience, the head and not the tail of my life situation.

I pray for the soon return of Jesus, I feel His return is really close. I know that He will come like a thief in the night – but I am informed. That big toe which was still dangling in the water of the world is now plucked out. I am all His and He knows it.

The only thing that I can take out of this world are those to whom the Lord in His grace has allowed me to be an instrument. Those souls may be saved not only by prayer and deliverance but by intercession.

In faith I have booked to return to Penang again in December 1990. It is the first time I will have returned for two consecutive years. Two weeks after my return I shall be teaching the ministry of deliverance and ministering in Denmark. Then I shall go on to Israel two months later. It is wonderful to see how God makes it all possible and to be able to plan in faith.

"Go and Do Likewise" took three years to write. This book took three months! That is a miracle in itself – and most of it was done fasting on water.

Stanley Vokes, an eloquent preacher, was addressing a small local church I attended recently. He gave us a wonderful, exhorting us into action for Jesus, sermon. He concluded "You are required to be pillars of the Church, not caterpillars crawling all over the ground!" I may be accused of many things but I do not think I could be accused of that!

During the three months of writing this book I really had to wrestle with the severe osteoporosis with which I was diagnosed following my accident. In Jerusalem in May 1990 I took myself off the medication in faith that I had received the word in Isaiah 58:10-11 to make fat (strong) my bones. "*And if thou draw out thy soul to the hungry, and satisfy the afflicted soul; then shall thy light rise in obscurity, and thy darkness be as the noon day: And the Lord shall guide thee continually, and satisfy thy soul in drought, and make fat thy bones: and thou shalt be like a watered garden, and like a spring of water, whose waters fail not.*"

I felt that I had first received a rhema at "The Battle Belongs to the Lord" conference arranged by Ellel Grange at Brighton early in 1990, for someone with disintegrating bones. Osteroporosis is brittle bone disease, so I claimed that word for my healing which came from the precious Bill Subritzky. I experienced many trials and testing of my faith, much pain and discomfort as I attempted to walk in what I had received.

I wrote to Bill, who was certain that a childhood curse needed to be dealt with. My bone pain went back to the age of eleven, my father had spoken a curse over me that he wished I had never been born and it witnessed in my spirit. Bill said to make certain I had forgiven my parents and that I honoured them, and I knew I had long ago met with this condition.

As I waited for the right moment to receive ministry it came unexpectedly after my last teach-in on September 1st 1990. It had been an incredible ministry for at least thirty of those present after the Word had gone forth and we all felt the power of the risen Christ and the anointing of the Holy Spirit as never before.

Angela was led by the Holy Spirit to pray the whole of Isaiah 58 over me. I realised as she prayed that if I were like a watered garden with a never failing spring my bones could not be dry or brittle. I was slain in the Spirit and as I lay there I experienced two things astonishingly, the love of God the Father for me His child and the wholehearted love of the Body of Christ around me.

I was healed and I knew it. The manifestation of the healing came forth, no pain, no discomfort, a strengthening of my bones, the erasing from my mind of this disease and its threatenings. A few weeks later as I fasted on water only for seven days, I shed about ten years and I felt new bones going into my frame. I am convinced without doubt that by His stripes I am healed, and I testify to this fact. My youth has been restored like the eagle's (Psalm 103:5) and the Lord has renewed my strength so I am mounting up like an eagle, I'm going against the storm and the wind, into it and I am an overcomer with renewed strength. *"I shall run and not be weary, I shall walk and not faint."* (Isaiah 40:31)

My prayer for you all is that this book, written from my heart will encourage, uplift and teach you to wield that sword of the Spirit and stick the enemy with it and to seek for holiness above all things.

Please cover the Christian Clinic For Environmental Medicine and its occupants with the blood of the Lamb, our precious Lord Jesus Christ.

Chapter 38

Weep For Jerusalem

I did get back to Penang in December 1990 – returning in early January 1991. Again against all the odds of raising my fare and organising a flight at the last moment, the Lord did both miraculously.

The Lord sent me to Penang for one special person. I believe humbly, and so does the man himself, that I was sent to save him from destruction. He was someone I had met on a previous visit and about whom the Lord had spoken to me in a very strong way, that this man was anointed by God for a very special purpose. I had heard many in the Full Gospel Assembly of Penang say the same thing.

I could write a complete book on my first encounter with heroin withdrawal and all its ramifications. Yet again I found myself coming against witchcraft. I was engaged also in a spiritual warfare involving a terrible spoken curse, and deception which had brought about the whole horrific and totally unexpected business. The first seven nights I had only a few hours sleep as I battled with the devil.

I saw yet again the mercy of the Lord and the power of the sword of the Spirit and the Blood of the Lamb. I was also quite wretched with a fever that lasted for three weeks, although I did not succumb to it.

I was tired and exhausted in every sense, yet with an anointing so strong it had to be God – because in the natural I could not hold myself up, especially in such tropical heat!

Such situations remove from us any ideas that we may

be doing anything in our own strength! Many were healed and set free and Jesus glorified, in particular on New Year's Day when I taught members of the Church at Goshen and ministered from 5.30pm – 3.30am the next morning, with only ten minutes break and half a glass of water!

It was a part of my ministry to teach others to pray for the peace of Jerusalem at every opportunity. (Psalm 122).

I arrived home tired, elated in the Spirit, but quiet in the natural. I travelled home lost in awe and wonder at the Father's love. I kept remembering how in Jerusalem in May 1990 I had been caused to sing "I stand, I stand in awe of You" throughout the streets, at the top of Mount Carmel, on the Mount of Olives, in fact, everywhere I set my feet in the land of Israel.

With just two weeks at home I prepared for my visit to Denmark to teach and minister to Women's Aglow.

Women's Aglow Fellowship International is a world-wide interdenominational organisation of renewed Christian women who are committed to Jesus Christ as Lord. Under the protective counsel of Christian leaders in each country, Aglow Fellowships meet in local groups on all five major continents.

Aglow, however, is much more than this simple statement. It is women . . . ministering to women; . . . fellowshipping together; . . . worshipping, praising and glorifying God in all areas of life; . . . coming to a full knowledge of Jesus Christ as Saviour, Lord, Baptiser, Deliverer and Healer . . . working for spiritual unity among all Christian believers . . . encouraging other women to be active members of their local churches . . . learning their unique rôle and their many creative opportunities according to Scripture.

The National President of Denmark had been told by the Holy Spirit that I was to be invited to set the captives free. Of course, she had never heard of me until someone gave her my book "Go and Do Likewise." So, after checking me out she telephoned me, telling me that she was under Holy Spirit instructions.

She did not tell me she checked up on me until later!! She also told me that the book ministered to her in several personal areas.

Just as I had explained to the members of the Church in Penang, I explained to the gathering of leaders in authority in Denmark that I would be praying for Israel before every session and as led by the Holy Spirit. The gulf war had broken out the day I left England (17.1.91) and so was on everyone's mind.

As I entered the hall to address these women I was deeply moved in my spirit to sense that these were no ordinary women. I would guess their ages ranged from about thirty to seventy. They had a special stamp of holiness; they were all anointed in a very real sense. Many had counselling or deliverance ministries or were on the Board of Women's Aglow. I felt I was on a very special mission to set the captives free.

Following one hour's praise and worship I taught from 9.30 am on the Saturday to 4.00 am on the Sunday morning. I had still not recovered from the Penang fever. I was extremely tired, having squeezed in a lot of catching-up during those few days between flights. Every bone in my body ached. I was attacked in my spine, my ribs, my hip and my neck!

I gave the teach-in contained in this book to a very receptive audience, hungry for the truth to set them free. Ending the teaching with the 'freedom from curse' prayer I began individual ministry. I should say before I even began teaching, the Holy Spirit told me, and I passed the joyful news on to them all in advance, that each person present was going to be set free in a very mighty way that weekend.

I truly never experienced the presence of the Holy Spirit in such a way. He was just there at my elbow; we talked all the time. He taught and instructed me with such clarity. Several times I actually stopped ministering so I could consult Him, I fell in love with Him over and over again!

Waiting on a word of knowledge or vision for each person, I ministered individually to some twenty ladies, beginning with the National President.

It was suggested that since we all had to get up again in a very few hours we should conclude. At 4.30 am, totally drained, I found myself drinking hot chocolate from a vending machine with the National President. We were both exhausted and although very tired I had such a peace.

Tove was concerned that there was no way I could minister to fifty four women in a morning that day! The place was actually closed down after lunch. Many had trains and ferries to catch, long journeys to make home.

As we trundled back to our dormitories I told her, "Don't worry, I've got to have a chat to the Holy Spirit and He'll tell me what to do."

I sat on the edge of my bed. It was now 5.30 am, I needed to rise at 6.30 am in order to pray. "Go to sleep," He said, "I'll advise you in the morning." I set my alarm on for 7.30 am. I thought it better to miss breakfast. Prising my eyes open with cold water bathing, I began earnest conversation with the Holy Spirit. He said, "I'll tell you when you are in the hall." During the praise I was in the front row to the side and did not normally move up front until it stopped. I was caused, however, to move out slightly to the side and turn and raise my hand in blessing over the women.

I was particularly looking at those I had already ministered to, the twenty set free. Such joy on their faces made me feel so incredibly happy. I was revelling in this delight when a voice said. "Weep for Jerusalem." I knew it to be a command from the Father and I told Him I simply could not weep, I was so happy. He repeated,

"Weep for Jerusalem" I entreated Him. "Look at those women set free in the name of your Son. How can I weep?" Again the command, "Weep for Jerusalem"

"Father," I told Him, "There is not a tear in me. If you want me to weep – then cause me to weep."

At this moment the women had moved into singing in the Spirit. Their melody was exquisite, and as it died down their pianist, (apparently trained at the Music Academy, but she had given her music to the Lord for His purposes) played with incredible pathos and I started to weep.

It was travail from the very depth of my being. I wept in the Spirit; it went on and on. I knew that my make-up had gone, mascara was running down my face, but I was doubled up, staggering from side to side clutching my stomach as I travailed. I couldn't even reach for a handkerchief! I felt that I had cried every tear I ever had inside and a lot I didn't have! Some were brought into deep repentance for not praying for Jerusalem over the years. I received numerous comments of this conviction from others later.

The travail ended in the only way possible – through the supernatural intervention of the Holy Spirit.

My very precious interpreter, also named Tove, was concerned for my appearance as we took the podium together. "Your mascara," she touched my cheek. "I'm not worried about my face, neither is my Father," I told her as I wiped it quickly with a tissue.

Through swollen eyelids I peered at them. They were bathed in light and peace.

Actually I did not want to teach, even to speak. I was lost in awe and wonder at His might, majesty, dominion and power.

I prayed for Jerusalem – and consulted the Holy Spirit.

He told me to line up the women into three rows of eighteen with approximately two to three feet between the rows and a gap at each end, to place seventeen of those ministered to at their rear and three to stand with me, including the interpreter.

I have a minute blue glass stoppered bottle for anointing. It is about the size of an old English penny and about a quarter inch in depth. I suddenly remembered as I reached for it that I had not refilled it from the night before. I was astonished to find that it had in fact refilled itself supernaturally. That tiny bottle was not empty even after anointing a further twenty people in a suburb on the Sunday evening. Ninety four people in all! I was quite overawed at this realisation.

The Holy Spirit led me to pray out root spirits; many common spirits like fear, anger and pride. Having exhaled about thirty common demons apiece during which time many wept or fell to the ground or did both, I then had to get them all to their feet again and I was given less common spirits to come against, like lesbianism, incest, warmongering, mocking, clown and jester, and know-all spirits.

As I received the discernment through words of knowledge, the Holy Spirit took me to the individual concerned. I was amazed, but I felt so close to Him, almost grafted into Him. That is the only way I can describe the closeness. More tears, laughter and manifestations, and when that was all over the Holy Spirit told me to get them to line up in one row and pass before me for anointing in the name of Jesus.

As I did so I was to say "I anoint you in the name of Jesus Christ, your Lord and Saviour. Receive your complete healing and deliverance now in His name."

All but four went down, some appeared unconscious, some rolled with laughter. The Holy Spirit caused me to bless and lay hands on the foetus of three who were pregnant and each one present had my hand laid on their heart and received the anointing of the Balm of Gilead. There had been so much brokenheartedness to deal with, so much grief. I said at the onset that these women were extraordinarily special holy anointed women. In the main they did not portray faces of agony or despair, but rather the radiance of Christ Jesus, permeating their faces.

I saw in them the reflection of myself. I should not be surprised. Here was another potent example of the saints in the Body covering up the most appalling hurts

212

and sores. And why? Because ignorance abounds in a majority of our churches concerning ancestral incest, exorcism, evil spirits, setting the captives free with our God-given authority and disobedience of God's commands.

On the Sunday evening I was to address a group of twenty who were in a dead Baptist church. They had all been baptised in the Holy Spirit and were desirous of knowing what to do next.

The National President's handsome and personable son was one of those deeply touched by the Holy Spirit and intensely desirous of being obedient.

I got back to Tove's flat totally spent. Her son was the chauffeur. I didn't know how I could tell him I was too tired to go to the house and minister, or advise, or do anything at all. I was aching all over, my whole being cried out for sleep. He even had to pull off my boots because I was too stiff to bend over!

I concluded reluctantly that I would see what the Holy Spirit said and asked Tove to wake me in two hours time. I fell fast asleep, not having been able to get a Word, and was awakened by a gentle but unwelcome tapping on my door!

Tove was so apologetic. She too was exhausted. "Please don't be pressurised. It's such an important time. We're sure the Lord brought you here but only you can decide."

I was jolly sure He had too! I yawned, sat up in bed, and took my Bible off the bedside table. It fell open on my lap. I read, *"Awake, awake; put on thy strength."* (Isaiah 52:1)

I groaned, got up and dressed.

By this time I hardly knew who I was! I was almost functioning by remote control. And yet, I was so weak, but I had an inner strength and peace and trust which can come only from being close to God. The Holy Spirit was holding me up.

As we entered the hallway of the property I could

hear angelic praise. I felt electrified by it. I looked at Tove "We did right to come," I said. I did ask if I could sit down. I told them that I hadn't the slightest idea what the Holy Spirit was going to do. They were loving and patient. I felt sorry for Tove as she had to be the interpreter now.

I spoke for two hours and ministered to each person getting incredible words of knowledge. One was a man I did not know who was a former Mason, really stubborn and angry, rejecting absolutely that he should get rid of his Masonic ring. According to his fellowship gathered he was very resistant to doing so. He also had a problem with his fingers.

Following my bringing what the Lord had said to him, that he would be used mightily, but it was conditional to ridding himself of a precious object, (it could be a piece of jewellery, I informed him), I had no idea that shortly afterwards he slipped out and flushed his Masonic ring down the loo! When he was slain in the Spirit later I was to come against curses on his throat and heart. Remember that Masons have a dagger to their heart and a noose around their neck when they invoke some of their abominable curses over themselves.

That night I preached on the blasphemy against the Holy Spirit, amongst other things. I was amazed! I had no idea I knew how to bring this Word. But the teacher, the guide, the comforter, the friend, He undertook. Bless Him, He undertook in all those areas for me during my time in both Penang and Denmark.

The Word to these brothers and sisters was to "come out and form their own Church of the Holy Spirit." This was agreed on.

Due to the war in the gulf I travelled home on a plane almost to myself. I was delighted not to have hubbub surround me. I sat back in my seat. "Father, I cannot pray, not even in the Spirit. I cannot read the Bible, I cannot think, I can only sit here and be in awe and wonder of You."

The taxi driver from the airport virtually had to carry me in from the cab. I thought I would never recover my strength – but within two days I was ministering at the Clinic after a hectic day with patients.

I got home Monday evening and on the Saturday a patient brought me three teaching tapes on Spiritual Warfare by Peter Horrobin of Ellel Grange – they were recorded on 16.1.91.

As I am always saying there is no co-incidence in the realm of the supernatural. It is all God-incidence. The patient was emphatic. I should play them *at once*! and I fully intended not to do so immediately. However the Holy Spirit intervened and on the Saturday night I lay back in bed listening to them, proclaiming "Amen! Amen!" There was also a tremendous teaching on intercession by a lady called Madeline.

She was confirming "Weep for Jerusalem", and Peter was talking about the "awe of the Lord" and the need for the members of the Body of Christ to stop lobbing hand grenades at one another. Satan loves this. He spoke that many churches were more concerned with what you did ten years ago than with the anointing you had at present!! He said there is no holy democracy yet churches will spend ten years having committee meetings to get a unanimous decision what to do and never actually do anything at all. The message was that God is not concerned with jumble sales, or what colour the church carpet should be, but with obedience to the Great Commission. His concern is that we actually get on with it.

If, reading this book, you are debating whether or not to come out of a church that is dead or stale or a church that is socially orientated to coffee mornings, a bless-me club, dinner parties to share criticism and gossip about members of the church then these are the tapes for you! The cassettes are available from Ellel Grange, Ellel, Near Lancaster, LA2 0HN.

On these tapes Peter speaks of the ongoing anointing

as being the blessing of obedience. I felt that was exactly what I was experiencing. Certainly since I got back from Denmark I have moved out into yet another Spiritual dimension. I do not pretend to understand what it is at present, only to say that I am surrounded with such a peace in spite of many pressures upon me. I know it is another stage of overcoming in the strength of the Lord and the reality that really there is none of me left.

Please pray for the work of the Clinic and my physical strength as I continue to walk in faith and obedience.

"If I forget thee, O Jerusalem, let my right hand forget her cunning. If I do not remember thee, Let my tongue cleave to the roof of my mouth; if I prefer not Jerusalem above my chief joy." (Psalm 137:5-6).

"For the rod of the wicked shall not rest upon the lot of the righteous; lest the righteous put forth their hands unto iniquity." (Psalm 125:3).

"Pray for the peace of Jerusalem: they shall prosper that love thee." (Psalm 122:6).

NOTE:

If, having read this book, you feel that we can help you, either physically or Spiritually or both, please do not hesitate to contact us. Should you require the Clinic papers please send a stamped addressed envelope to:

The Christian Clinic for Environmental Medicine
Lane End
Highlands Lane
Westfield
Woking
Surrey GU22 9PU
England